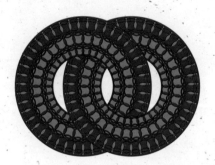

DESCENT

DESCENT

SELECTED ESSAYS, REVIEWS, AND LETTERS

John Haines

CavanKerry ❖ Press LTD.

CavanKerry Press Ltd.
Fort Lee, New Jersey
www.cavankerrypress.org

Library of Congress Cataloging-in-Publication Data

Haines, John Meade, 1924-
Descent : selected essays, reviews, and letters / John Haines.
p. cm.
ISBN-13: 978-1-933880-18-1 (alk. paper)
ISBN-10: 1-933880-18-X (alk. paper)
1. Haines, John Meade, 1924---Authorship. 2. Poetry--History and > criticism. 3.
Haines, John Meade, 1924---Homes and haunts--Alaska. 4. Haines, John Meade,
1924---Correspondence. 5. Poets, American--20th century--Biography. I. Title.

PS3558.A33A6 2010
809.1--dc22
2009049911

Cover photograph Dorothy Alexander © 2010

First Edition 2010, Printed in the United States of America

Contents

Contents

ALASKA: STORIES AND REVIEWS

POETRY CHRONICLES

MEMOIRS

Preface

The various essays and reviews collected here represent what may be a closing period in my life as a writer, as poet and critic. As has been the case since I began writing in my early twenties, Alaska, the land and its history, its people and culture, continues to be a main focus in my writing. And there is always that other element in the background: our human history on this planet Earth, the harm we have done and continue to do as witnessed in Mythology, the Art and Literature we have left behind us. My paper on the *Gilgamesh* story bears witness to this in a very personal way, as do my thoughts on writing, on our current social and political climate, represented perhaps most intensely in my late *Wartime* memoir, the story of my US Navy service in WW II, an experience that has served as a lesson in my thinking, and remained a potential material for my writing.

I have especially appreciated the *Poetry Chronicles* assigned to me by the editor of *The Hudson Review*, and more recently the welcome I have met with at *The Sewanee Review*, for my Memoir essays, the three of them included in this collection. I have many friends and fellow writers to thank for their support of my work; former students and faculty with whom I have remained friends; my early homestead years that taught me so much and established the ground of my life as poet; the many writers, poets and novelists, classical and modern, whose thought and work nourished me in difficult times, setting an example I might follow.

I would like to thank Baron Wormser for his generous introduction for this book, and others at CavanKerry Press who helped make it possible. I hope to have another book, whether in verse or prose, before my time runs short, when I must set my pen aside and, as we sometimes say: "close the book."

John Haines, 24 July 2009

Introduction

This volume bears witness to John Haines's position as a true man of letters. The essays, reviews, chronicles, memoirs, comments and poems (spanning over four decades) testify to the breadth and depth of his concerns. The life—rooted for decades in Alaska—and the writing are bound together inextricably. Haines speaks for the land and the land speaks to Haines. It is that simple and that complex, that joyful and that rueful.

Increasingly, we can see that the premise of any meaningful discourse about anything first must take into account life on earth—that which sustains and that which endangers. This might seem self-evident to anyone at any time but life on earth tends to be the first thing that civilization takes for granted. There have been cities to build, religions to elaborate, sciences to discover, technologies to hone and arts to create. The premise has been that the earth will take care of itself and, indeed, it will. How human beings are connected with this caring is another question and one that looms larger every day. To live on the earth as something more than a user is a charge that has occupied Haines's days and works.

Haines is foremost a poet, one for whom poetry is the primal call that connects language with the earth. To a world that looks at the earth as a resource and that views poetry as a medium distinguished primarily by stylistic ticks—two views that go hand in deadening hand—a voice such as Haines's may appear beside the point. This would be a serious misapprehension; Haines's regard for the connections between the earth and poetry stems from the chthonic impulses that gave birth to poetry to begin with, that elemental rapture of physical spirit.

This is not to make him a shaman or any such figure. Romanticizing older cultures is of no interest to him nor is arrogating spiritual insight that must be dearly and slowly won. What interests Haines throughout the various modes represented in this volume is to clear away the numerous confusing, self-justifying and downright mendacious vapors that surround various human projects—be it drilling for oil or writing poems. He is a critic in the pure sense—a truth teller who has no use for relativism. As he puts it, "A river is more than water flowing." It takes a poet to say that, one whose voice is unimpeded by the calculations that drive corporate pragmatism, to say nothing of greed.

The work of poetry is to restore the depths of meaning to language. For Haines that depth emanates from our living on earth. We are part of the great family of dependent creatures. The poet's responsibilities—a topic of great importance to Haines and one to which this volume bears eloquent testimony—have little to do with the buzzing literary world. Rather they are the responsibilities of one who treasures language and inspiration and who seeks to find the means to help us find the fullness that we know is in each moment of our lives on this planet whose richness is literally incredible. They are the responsibilities of one who realizes that poetry is much more than a vocal decoration. In its rapt attentiveness poetry ever courts wisdom.

In the meantime we stumble along and Haines is unsparing about those stumbles. He has never courted favor but he has never constructed an armor from his ideals. I think of all those days and nights in that homestead south of Fairbanks, or the profound dwelling that he did and took such a deep hold on him. We come and go on the face of the earth—that is our fate but how we do it is everything. In the pieces collected herein—pieces taken from the pages of newspapers and literary journals, pieces that were forewords to books and talks to conferences—Haines's voice is true and clear. It is an intensely American voice in the sense that it insists we can be connected to the land in ways that may redeem and vivify us. It insists that the place of poetry is central not peripheral. It is rooted in memories that come from one man's life and memories that are the dream life of the earth. If, as I believe, the poets who will endure are the poets who have something genuine to impart to us, then Haines is one who will endure. This volume adds to the trove that he has bequeathed us.

Baron Wormser

OTHER BOOKS BY JOHN HAINES

POETRY

Winter News, 1966

The Stone Harp, 1971

Twenty Poems, 1971

Cicada, 1977

News from the Glacier, 1980

New Poems, 1990

Where the Twilight Never Ends, 1994

At the End of This Summer, 1997

Collected Poems, 1993, 1996

For the Century's End, 2001

Of Your Passage, O Summer, 2004

PROSE

Living Off the Country, 1981

Of Traps and Snares, 1981

Other Days, 1982

Stories We Listened To, 1986

The Stars, The Snow, The Fire, 1986, 2000

Fables and Distances, 1996

NOTABLE VOICES
CavanKerry❖Press

CavanKerry Press is proud to publish the works
of established poets of merit and distinction.

CavanKerry Press is grateful for the support it
receives from the New Jersey State Council on the Arts.

NATIONAL
ENDOWMENT
FOR THE ARTS

This project is supported in part by an award from
the National Endowment for the Arts.

DEDICATION

I wish to dedicate this book to the memory of my good friend and colleague, Professor Roy Bird, at the University of Alaska, Fairbanks. To many of my former students in the University Honors Program, for their appreciation of my efforts as teacher on their behalf. And to my dear friend, Anita Stelcel, for her companionship in this late time of my life. My thanks to all.

I

DESCENT

Descent

Why we do a certain thing rather than another, when it would seem that a number of choices lie open to us, can be matter for a lifetime of thought, and we would still not have arrived at a final answer.

In my student days in New York, in the early 1950s, when I was far from any sort of mature work or outlook, still puzzling out my life from day to day and from month to month, the reading I had undertaken ranged through the whole of modern poetry in English, with initial forays into Spanish and German poetry, as well as the better part of modern and classical literature generally—the novels, the short stories and plays, along with the many critical commentaries. For reasons easily understood, considering my earlier venture to Alaska, that reading included also a good deal of work from Scandinavian literature—from Sweden, Iceland, Norway, and Denmark—and I refer here to the work of writers like Knute Hamsun, Jens Peter Jacobsen, and Sigrid Undset.

Amid all of this reading and study, there was one text above all that gained a life interest for me, and that was William Carlos Williams's *In the American Grain*. It is an idiosyncratic collection of essays on American history, influenced certainly by D.H. Lawrence's *Studies in Classic American Literature*, a book it closely resembles, and the essays range from Discovery through Colonial times, focusing now and again on figures like Daniel Boon, Aaron Burr, and Samuel Houston, who were, or seemed to be, at odds with the prevailing winds of conquest and settlement.

The main theme of the book is the discovery, if only potential, of that true ground underfoot—the one inherent thing in our history, discounted then as now by all but a few. And the essay that in many respects held the most enduring interest for me was a brief thing of four pages called "Descent." Its substance can be felt in the following quotation:

> "The primitive destiny of the land is obscure . . . .
> Through that stratum of obscurity the frail
> genius of the place must penetrate.
>
> I speak of esthetic satisfaction. This want,
> in America, can only be filled by knowledge,
> a poetic knowledge of that ground."

And elsewhere in that essay I found this potent instruction: "It is imperative that we sink."

I took those words, and others like them, literally as well as symbolically; they seemed at the time to be meant for me alone. When I returned to Alaska in 1954, to my home region of Richardson, still isolated nearly seventy miles by road from Fairbanks, I made the decision—though I could not have articulated it then as I do now—to let go, to sink into that country, accept it on its own terms, and make of it what I could. Among those steep hills of birch and aspen, on the fire-scarred spruce ridges and windswept domes, in the bogs and alder-tangled creek bottoms; in the Tanana River islands, sandbars, and channels; in the early snowfall and late spring, the long nights of midwinter and the long light of midsummer—in its scattered, transitory human history also—I found my place in which to settle, in the true sense, and everything has grown from that.

As it was the Interior of that country—closed in by the Alaska Range to the south, by the Arctic Range to the north, and by the many domes and ridges of the inter-lying hills—so it was my own interior I set out to explore, with the aid of a few books and with the countryside itself open before me: that esthetic ground from which all art and literature draw their nourishment, a soil in its own right and, unlike this material earth, inexhaustible.

I might have settled elsewhere and become a different man and writer. The decision was, if you will, in part accident, or it may have been governed by that thing we call fate. I have responded at one time or another to the seashore, to its tidal pools and unique forms of aquatic life; and to the rocks and painted caves of a semi desert mountain complex. The woodlands of the eastern United States have appealed to me in another way, both familiar and strange in their own right. Not long ago, returning to Fairbanks by road from Anchorage, we drove over a rough mountain pass where the countryside, incredibly green with mosses and late summer shrubs, and with numerous outcroppings of rock, reminded me strongly of the Yorkshire Moors and the Scottish Highlands, a countryside I had come to know insufficiently during a year's stay in northern England. There too in a land long settled, bearing the marks of an older pastoral society, a part of me came briefly to feel at home.

But beyond all of these lay that apparently inevitable, to-be-discovered region, the boreal forest; and beyond that, the open distance of that landscape left behind by the ice fields, and from which, in the course of a dozen thousand years or so, much of the rest has come.

From where does it come, this felt familiarity, of land and space? I do not know for a certainty, though I have more than once attempted to define it. In a letter written years ago to a fellow writer, I expressed it in the following way:

> When we look out on that high and open tundra with its scattered ponds and grassy mounds, I think our attention to it has little to do with an ideal, but rather with a memory, so embedded in our consciousness that we respond to it without quite understanding why. If, as I believe, that landscape corresponds to an original setting for humanity and if in some part of ourselves we have remained open to it, then our response to the land has a sensible explanation; and imagination, released by those contours and details, awakens, and the mind finds a true home for a moment.

I believe this to be close to the truth, and as close as we are likely to get.

But to descend implies that one must eventually climb, emerge from that place of descent, bearing whatever gift or insight one may have gained. After years of instructive isolation in that interior country I returned, to reenter that other life I had left behind and had almost forgotten. And I have, not without initial difficulty, come to accept and like the city where I find it, a walkable and convenient place to be, with its own character, necessary to humanity as any stonewalled field or neighboring copse.

So much, briefly, for my own natural history. Meanwhile, and always, there is that other America—the persistent face of wealth and privilege, of ownership and political hierarchy; this self-devouring enterprise that admits no limits to its conquest of nature, to its right to exploitation of every known resource, and which even now refuses to restrain its appetite. This industrial maggot burrowing into the "last frontier," as if a people could not rest and thrive if that American mirage, the frontier, ceased to exist. But it is already disappearing, exists perhaps now as a kind of tinted vacationland, an immense outdoor theater. And I believe we will learn to live with its absence or perish, as a nation, as a people.

In writing this, I recall the provocative concluding sentence of Williams' essay: "However hopeless it may seem, we have no other choice: we must go back to the beginning; it must all be done over."

Consider those words as you will—in the sense of a history to be retold with a firmer affection for the truth, as I think Williams intended, and as difficult as it may seem and will always be. That is the task of the writer, the poet, the artist; and of all of us who in one way or another labor to make of this damaged but still resilient earth a saner and better place.

And once again, and with my own experience in mind, beyond most of our fleeting temporal concerns, lies that other, parallel country of imagination, that knows no geographical or political boundaries, and where a writer, a poet, is free to roam to settle and build as he can.

1995

ON POETRY AND POETS

The Theme of Loss, of Sorrow and Redemption in Gilgamesh

I have taken as my text the story of Gilgamesh, with its theme of transgression against the forest Gods, of punishment, and eventual reconciliation. It is a theme repeated in one form or another throughout much of classical literature, and echoed in Coleridge's *Ancient Mariner*, that "sadder and wiser man." Sorrow is at the heart of it, and if it ends not in joy but in understanding and some form of redemption, that much at least may console us.

My interest in the subject is not primarily academic, but intensely personal, in that many years ago I lived out a part of the story in the wilderness of Alaska, as a homesteader and hunter. When, years later, I first read a translation of Gilgamesh, I knew that in some way I was reading of my own life and, indeed, the life of humanity. For it is a universal story, one we re-enact over and over in our still unresolved war against Nature. In a brief essay published in *Amicus Journal* in 1996 I had this to say:

> The old stories of antiquity, the myths and legends, the adventures of gods and heroes, continue to be a true guide to the human story; in returning to them we return to a source. In the epic of Gilgamesh, for example, we find the archetypal

11

story of offense against Nature . . . . the consequences of which we continue to share, though we have other names now for the forces involved.

Most of us, I think, know the story of Gilgamesh, the Sumerian King and hero, and his search for understanding and at least a partial redemption, following on his killing of the forest guardian, Humbaba, and the death of his friend and companion, Enkidu: the pain, the sorrow, the anger and bewilderment; and then his long pilgrimage in search of help from one source or another.

Some, readers and scholars, have found in the story something personal and humanly true, as is the case with many of the stories of antiquity. My own reading, as I have said, has been particularly personal, and with at times a degree of intensity not easily conveyed to a weekend recreational hunter, though I did not for many years understand or sense the parallel between my own adventure and that of Gilgamesh.

I will not, then, rehearse for you all of the history of the epic: from the discovery of the text, in stone so to speak, in Nineveh in the mid-nineteenth century. Most of this can be read in the numerous notes to translations of the epic, and in the immense scholarship that has followed. What concerns me here is the underlying vitality of the story, and my own experience of it as a young man living in the wilderness of Interior Alaska. A complete account of that life would require more than the time allotted for this paper; I have, however, written of it in both poems and prose, a few selections from which I will read to you in the course of my presentation.

The different versions of the epic have more or less been resolved into the one we know today, rendered for us in many English translations; and I would mention here those by authors like David Ferry, Herbert Mason, and Noah Kramer. What remains to us, when all the details of death, of loss and renewal are set aside, is that eternal, still modern story of offense to Nature, and for which we pay a lasting penalty. The story and its meaning for us takes on a contemporary importance in the light of our ongoing argument between the forces of economic expansion, and the conservation of resources, of wilderness management, and so fourth, to make use of accepted terms that by no means adequately express the significance of the story for us now.

During an early period of the wilderness life I once knew, I wrote a number of poems in which I sought to embody something of what I was living through and coming to know. I will read one of these at this time, simply as an example of my struggle to understand and make clearer to myself the life I had chosen to live, and in a form I could acknowledge.

> Tree of my life
> you have grown slowly
> in the shadows of giants.
>
> Through darkness and solitude
> you stretch year by year
> toward that strange, clear light
> in which the sky is hidden.
>
> In the quiet grain of your
> thoughts the inner life
> the forest stirs
> like a secret still to be named.
> ("The Tree")

That "secret still to be named" has been at the heart of a quest for a further knowledge and understanding. At best, perhaps, this cannot finally be named. We know it when we see it, and feel ourselves a part of it.

In reference to the world of Gilgamesh, we are speaking of a time when people did not easily distinguish between the human individual and a force in Nature which that individual might represent. Thus, in our particular text, and in much of ancient art and culture, we encounter a sort of cosmic confusion, with the gods and heroes, male and female, working things out on a vast, epic scale—a world of rich imagination as well as of observable fact, rich in poetry and story, that kept the world alive in the sense of a spiritual continuity assumed to lie at the heart of things, and that it all had meaning.

We speak today in terms of "bio-diversity," of "eco-systems," and "threatened species," and so forth. We understand what is meant by these abstract terms, but they have none of the resonance of the ancient poetry of mythology, rich and storied as it was and remains to the reader and listener awake to the drama and the meaning of it: a parallel reality equal in its own way to the scientific explanations we have grown accustomed to in modern times.

We are now much occupied with ecology and its various sub-categories of study and application. This sort of thing, as necessary as it must be for us at this time, becomes a kind of abstract pseudo-religion. Aside from its immediate practicality, it speaks to a profound need in our nature, for belief in and love of the world we inhabit.

There are in fact many themes at work in the epic of *Gilgamesh,* and I have emphasized only one, but it is one that seems to me to be at the heart of the story, and around which all others revolve. The story is about death, surely, and the loss of a friend and companion. But it is more than that, and something other, or so I feel. Many poets have felt in one way or another this sense of loss: of an early intuition of the world of Nature and one's abiding place within it; and with age and experience something of that spiritual bonding seems to have been lost, as expressed, for instance, in Wordsworth's "Intimations of

Immortality": "And yet I know, wher'ere I go, There has passed away a glory from the earth." Perhaps all of us, at one time or another, have been aware of something given us in childhood: an intuition of the world and of our potential place in it, that is all too often overgrown in the *business* of professional life and related activities. Some of us, at least, may at some point feel the need to return, to recover that original feeling, clichéd though it may be, expressed in that familiar phrase "back to nature," and which we repeat without understanding why.

That is to say: We have the story; it can be told, in one translation or another, discussed by scholars, and become part of what we call literature, the classics. And there is nothing amiss with that. But my concern is with some deeper truth, the lessons that lie in such old stories, and that I feel we need to relearn, and place them in a context of usefulness to us.

One dominant theme in the story is loss, certainly, but of what? For it represents, to my mind, a loss more complicated and lasting than most of us are aware of. It is easy for some in our time to criticize the activities and sometime excesses of our environmental groups in their efforts to rescue some portion of a threatened Nature in the face of an economic expansion that appears to have no limits. It may be worth pointing also to the tendency toward abstraction in describing those aspects of Nature we wish to save from further intrusion and destruction. Nature, for some, even the most dedicated, becomes at this point a specialization, among all too many such in our time.

But let me return for a moment to my own story. In leaving that wilderness life behind, as I did at the end of the 1960s, I could not have defined my reasons for doing so. I knew that a certain life in a loved place had mysteriously come to an end, and another was tentatively beginning, one I could not name. There was this deep sense of loss, or displacement, on the other hand, and on the other a sense of adventure in reentering a world of cities and of mass populations I had left behind many years before.

And it was, moreover, a lingering, obscure sense of loss that led me to return to that original scene, the Richardson Homestead, in the early 1980s, and which in turn led me, inevitably, to a reading of *Gilgamesh*. When, for example, I read of his axe-blow on the cedar tree in order to call forth the great warden of the forest, Humbaba, I was reminded of my calling of a bull moose in hunting season: knocking with an axe on a tree trunk, or thrashing with a stick in the brush. I knew, from long practice, what it is to talk to a creature like a moose. That is, at the right time and in the appropriate season, to call, by voice or by other means, and have the creature respond with a thrashing of his horns in the brush, or by voice in answer. This was a practical matter at the time for someone whose livelihood depended on the success of the hunting season, but it was always intense with a mysterious watching and waiting that I somehow understood was part of an old ceremony: The hunter and his quarry come to terms with life and death. In that early period I wrote a poem in which I attempted to articulate my sense of this.

> Who are you,
> calling me in the dusk,
>
> O dark shape
> with heavy horns?
> I am neither cow
> nor bull—
> I walk upright
> and carry your death
> in my hands.
>
> It is my voice
> answers you,
>
> beckoning, deceitful,

ruse of the hunter . . . .

At twilight,
in the yellow frost

I wait for you.
("A Moose Calling")

And indeed I waited, many hours and many days, cold evenings and frost-lit mornings, for that other voice to respond. As intent as I was on the immediate need, I was also aware of participating in an ancient ritual. In a page from my memoir, *The Stars, The Snow, The Fire,** I phrased it in this way.

It was far, far back in time, that twilight country where men sometimes lose their way, become as trees confused in the shapes of snow. But I was at home there, my mind bent away from humanity, to learn to think a little like that thing I was hunting. I entered for a time the old life of the forest, became part fur myself.

And I went on, to conclude that portion of the memoir, as follows:

Sometime there may come to us in a depleted world the old hunter's dream of plenty. The rich country, full of game, fish and fur, bountiful as it once was. The bear, the moose, and the caribou. The woods are thick with rabbits, the marten crossing and recrossing, their paired tracks always going somewhere in the snow under the dark spruces. And carefully, one foot before the other, the round, walking track of the lynx: they never seem to hurry. Beaver in the ponds, a goshawk beating the late

---

*John Haines, *The Stars, The Snow, The Fire* (St. Paul, Graywolf Press, 1989)

winter thickets like a harrying ghost; and now and then the
vague menace of a wolf passing through. This, or its sometime
shadow: the country dead, and nothing to see in the snow.
Famine, and the great dream passing.

("Of Traps and Snares")

That "famine" I refer to may be spiritual as well as actual;
and the "great dream" is not merely that of the hunter, but of
us all.

I do not believe that what I have been speaking of here can
be dismissed as romanticism, though it surely contains elements
of that. I believe, that is, in a fundamental human truth in our
relation to what we call Nature, as abstracted as it has become in
our time; and this is why a story like *Gilgamesh* retains its force,
and with appropriate authority. Much the same might be said,
as we know, of such ancient tales as that of *Daphne and Apollo*,
or *Orpheus*, and of all such visions of a hero's spiritual journey
into the underworld, as we find it in Homer and in Virgil, and as
Dante has described it for us in his Comedia. The story remains
true, and all of us, to some degree, are required to relive it.

To repeat: The theme here is not, to my mind, to do with
death as such, nor with the loss of a friend, though these are
surely included in the story. It has, I feel, more to do with a
fundamental alienation from the world and from Nature, a fact
of which we are at times hardly aware, but perhaps increasingly
so in a diminished planetary space.

"Paradise Lost," indeed, we may say. In thinking of
Enkidu's alienation from his animal friends who turn away
from him, following on his first encounter with humanity.
Gilgamesh returns to his city and his people, to take up life
again in a subtly changed world, wiser perhaps for his ordeal,
his journey of sorrow. That much, it seems to me, can be hoped
for; and in that sometime sadness, or sorrow, a self-knowledge
may be gained, an earned wisdom; and there may be also, if not

18

Joy precisely, at least a reconciliation, an inner peace, of mind and conscience.

The redemption, I think we may say, can never be complete, but only partial, and for some of us, never permanent. It is, however, a quest we may never entirely abandon, for in it lies our best hope of salvation.

If I have achieved any wisdom in this life of Letters, perhaps it is embodied in a few poems I have written in recent years, and in a few pages of memoir and literary criticism. But more especially in a poem I wish to read to you in conclusion, and derived in great part from the Gilgamesh epic. There I was able, after several years of thought and writing, to bring together the essential lessons that lie in the epic and in my own experience. In doing so, I felt a certain deep satisfaction that I had not only completed a poem long worked on and with which I was formally pleased; I had additionally come to terms with something in my own nature, hidden for many years in doubt and confusion.

In the poem I shall read, titled "The Legend," the main characters are identified by name and the basic story is kept intact, though it is condensed into a few stanzas. You may recognize also one or two elements from another of our English classics. The poem, then, is in three parts.

I

I understand the story of Gilgamesh,
of Enkidu, who called the wind by name,
who drank at the pool of silence,
kneeling in the sunburnt shallows
with all four-footed creatures.

I know the name of that exile,
the form that it takes within us:

19

the parting and breaking of things,
the distance and anguish.

I know too, in its utter strangeness,
that whoever asks of the sun its rising,
of the night its moonstruck depths,
stirs the envy of God in his lofty cabin.

And when Enkidu awoke, called
from his changed, companionless sleep-
singly, in glittering pairs,
the beasts vanished from the spring.

II

The forest bond is broken,
and the tongued leaves no longer
speak for the dumb soul lost
in the wilderness of his own flesh.

Leopard, gazelle, insect and floating
leaf—all that had life for him:
the moon with her wandering children,
the storm-horse and the shepherd-bird,
become as salt to his outspread hand.

Let him go forth, to try the roads,
become that wasted pilgrim, familiar
with dust, dry chirps and whispers;
to die many times—die as a man dies,
seeing death in the life of things.

And then descend, deep into rootland –
not as a temple-gardener, planting

with laurel the graves of gods and heroes,
but as one grieving and lost . . . .

To ask of the dead, of their fallen
web-faces, the spider's truth,
the rove-beetle's code of conduct.
By such knowledge is he cured,
and lives to face the sun at evening,
marked by the redness of clay,
the whiteness of ash on his body.

III

By stealth, by the mastery of names,
and one resounding axe-blow
rung on the cedar-post at dawn,
the great, stomping bull of the forest
was slain. Rain only speaks
there now on the pelted leaves.

Overheard through the downpour,
in the stillness of my own
late-learned solace, I understand
through what repeated error
we were driven from Paradise.
The nailed gate and the fiery angel
are true.

Could we ask them,
speaking their wind-language
of cries, of indecipherable song,
it may be that the swallows
who thread the water at evening
would tell us; or that the sparrows

who flock after rain, would write
in the coarse yellow meal
we have strewn at the threshold,
why God gave death to men,
keeping life for himself.

For the strong man driven to question,
and for him who, equally strong,
believes without asking,
sleep follows like a lasting shadow.

1981-1996

Welcome to Apocalypse: The Poet as Prophet: Some Notes on Robinson Jeffers

I want to thank all of you for inviting me to this annual meeting. I feel honored, and I do not mean that in any casual sense. I want to particularly thank my friend, fellow poet, and critic Dana Gioia; and Arthur Coffin (who is not here, I'm sorry to say); Robert Zaller, Bob Brophy, Rob Kafka, John Hicks, and Alex Vardamis.

What I have to say this morning is no more than a sketch of something I hope to revise and amplify at a later date. Robinson Jeffers has long been one of my models in poetry, someone whose work I discovered at a fairly early age when I was just beginning to write seriously; he remains one of my lasting affections among modern poets.

I won't pretend to speak here as a scholar, one whose research empowers him to speak at length of Jeffers and in critical detail. I speak as a poet, one who has learned from Jeffers, as from many other poets, what the art at its best can be. I might say also that it would not be easy for me to speak of poetry, of Jeffers and his work, and avoid reference to this turn of the century and the prospects before us.

In considering what I might say of Jeffers at this time, and not avoid the stated theme of the conference, I've been drawn to a consideration of the poet as he appears in past literature as speaker to the people, whether as prophet in the classical, or biblical sense, or as dramatist of humanity's eternal struggle with the gods, with Nature, as well as with our human nature.

Whatever else I may have to say, there is little doubt in my mind that Jeffers is among the foremost of our modern poets, rare in any age, and in ours an outstanding figure. His dismissal by one of our Ivy League critics as "a West Coast nature poet," is not only a failure of critical judgment, but a kind of East Coast snobbery and an insult. And if any writer of our time can be said to embody in his work the theme of apocalypse, it is he.

Precisely when I first encountered Jeffers' work I cannot say, but I do recall reading him during my first year as a student in New York in 1950-1951. I recall also that he was being read by some of the young people I knew then, and I think his work was generally a part of the literary *culture of the time.* After I finished with my art studies in 1952, my first wife and I moved west to Monterey, drawn there mainly by Jeffers' example, to Carmel Valley, Big Sur, and the surrounding country. The valley, the coastline, were for us suffused with Jeffers and his writing, his poems and verse dramas.

Although my initial venture to Alaska after World War II had nothing directly to do with Jeffers (I had not read him, nor even heard of him), it does seem likely that his example lay in the back of my mind when I returned to the Richardson Homestead in 1954. I had then no program, no Hawk Tower to build, only an instinct as to what I wanted and needed to do—a vision, so to speak, requiring many years to clarify. Meanwhile, a life to live and work to do.

To what extent Jeffers influenced my own writing at an early stage would be hard to say now, though I sense in a few of my poems from the early 1950s something of his voice and verse style. One thing I can testify to is the force of his example, of his convictions and his stating of them. Here, for me at the time, was a poet who would speak openly and honestly on history, on politics and public life, and with no apparent regard to the consequences. This was for me a lesson, one I did not forget, though my writing has steered far afield from the example offered by Jeffers, moving stylistically in other directions under the influence of very different poets, such as T. S. Eliot, Ezra Pound, and W. C. Williams, as well as numerous poets in other languages.

What concerns me most immediately at this moment is the voice of the poet as prophet and teacher; the poet as social critic, as speaker to the people. And what I find so consistent in Jeffers' work, from beginning to end, is that prophetic note that can on occasion become monotonous, perhaps repetitious, but that also embodies a truth of our times to be found nowhere else.

There is that voice, in literature, in the classics, in the Bible—a *passion,* if you will, that empowers the text, that makes of it something more than a passing amusement, and mainly to be found in poetry, in verse, but also at times in certain works of fiction, and I would mention here as one prominent and neglected example the German writer Hermann Broch, and his major novels, *The Sleepwalkers* and *The Death of Virgil.*

What may be essential, and what is largely missing in poetry today, is that historical and philosophical perspective, to be gained mainly from a familiarity with the classics. I know that my own recent rereading of Greek and Roman history and literature has sharpened my sense of where we are at this moment in our history, teetering, as it were, between a faltering democracy and a kind of corporate imperialism. We have yet to see the outcome, but can perhaps admit the premonitions.

It is true of the classics, of all ancient texts and tales, that they embody the lasting truths of our human condition. To the extent that contemporary literature and art acknowledge this and learn from it, our poems and stories may survive the current market. I refer to that larger theme, so conspicuously absent from contemporary poetry. And it may be that in our modern era the proliferation of the public media has deprived the art of poetry of its older audience, and also of its ancient voice, that which speaks to us all.

To speak the truth as we see it: Nothing else can justify our claims to art, and the art of poetry. As Jeffers once put it, "I can tell lies in prose." Yet even there, in our prose criticism, we are bound to truth, and I cannot imagine Jeffers lying even in prose! Indeed, his one major critical essay, "Poetry, Gongorism, and a Thousand Years," demonstrates his need to speak directly and honestly. The gravity, the solemn authority in Jeffers' verse and prose—a quality that has all but disappeared from American writing:

> Therefore though not forgotten, not loved, in gray old
>   Years in the evening leaning
> Over the gray stones of the tower top,
> You shall be called heartless and blind;
> And watch new time answer old thought, not a face strange
>   Nor a pain astonishing.
>
> ("Soliloquy")

In my recent rereading of Jeffers I have discovered a number of parallels in the thought of writers like the Scottish poet Edwin Muir, and in a contemporary of mine, Hayden Carruth. I would like here to quote a few passages from Muir's prose writings. From an essay, "The Poetic Imagination":

> We live in a world created by applied science and our present is unlike the present of any other age . . . . Applied science shows us a world of constant mechanical progress . . . . machines give birth to ever new generations of machines, and the new machines are always better and more efficient than the old, and begin where the old left off . . . . but in the world of human beings all is

different; there we find no mechanical progress . . . . every human being has to begin at the beginning . . . . with the same difficulties, and pleasures, the same temptations, the same problems of good and evil, the same inward conflict, the same need to learn how to live, the same inclination to ask what life means.

(From *Essays on Literature and Society*, p. 226)

And from a passage in Muir's diaries of the late 1930s, we find this:

The nineteenth century thought that machinery was a moral force and would make men better . . . . how could the steam-engine make men better? If I look back over the last hundred years it seems to me that we have lost more than we have gained . . . . that what we have gained is trifling, for what we have lost was old and what we have gained is merely new. The world might have settled down into a passable Utopia by now if it had not been for "progress."

(*Extracts from a Diary*, 1937-1939)

Whether one agrees with all that Muir has to say here, I think his thought would find agreement with that of Jeffers in many respects. We can, for example, recall some lines and phrases from the poem "Science."

Man, introverted man. . . .

. . . .

Has begot giants, but taken up
Like a maniac with self-love and inward conflicts
    cannot manage his hybrids.

. . . .

Now he's bred knives on nature turns them also inward. . . .

. . . .

A little knowledge, a pebble from the shingle. . . .

. . . Who would have dreamed this
infinitely little too much?

Or, as Muir says at the conclusion of his essay, "The
Poetic Imagination:" "in spite of our machines, the habits
of the human heart remain what they have always been, and
imagination deals with them as no other faculty can."

I'd like at this point to quote from a couple of poems
recently published which I consider fairly typical of a good deal
of current verse writing. I will refrain from naming the authors.
From a recent issue of one of our prominent literary journals:

> On our long flight over the Atlantic
> the already drunk were served
> again and again their two little bottles
> of Scotch or vodka or whatever else
> they wanted—soon followed by another
> pair, and another—such cute miniatures
> that I wanted to save the bottles for children,
> and in fact tucked away a couple
> for that purpose, and one to use later
> for shaving lotion. . . .

And from a recent anthology, some lines of a more formal
variety:

> Dad pushed my mother down the cellar stairs.
> Gram had me name each plant in her garden.
> My father got drunk. Ma went to country fairs.
> The pet chameleon we had was warden
> of the living room curtains where us kids
> stood waiting for their headlights to turn in.

Let us compare these lines with some sample passages
from Jeffers:

Peace is the heir of dead desire,
Whether abundance killed the cormorant
In a happy hour, or sleep or death
Drowned him deep in dreamy waters,
Peace is the ashes of that fire,
The heir of that king, the inn of that journey.

("Suicide's Stone")

The tide, moving the night's
Vastness with lonely voices,
Turns, the deep dark shining
Pacific leans on the land,
Feeling his cold strength
To the outmost margins: You Night will resume
The stars in your time.

("Night")

Well, what is the difference here? On the one hand, in my first example, a simulated free verse that appears to have no more than the character of mediocre prose, and a near total absorption with a trivial incident in one's personal life. And to impose, superficially, as in my second example, a more formal order on the lines, hardly improves the general character of the verse.

And then, with Jeffers, an underlying cadence learned from an early study of classical poetry; a solemnity that comes from attention to the world at large, to our natural and historical background; a verse grounded in that eternal reality on which human life has always been grounded. Or perhaps we can say: It is the difference between poetry in the true sense of the word, and a sort of pastime imitation of it—a way of writing all too easily sanctioned by contemporary schools of verse. The better part of what is published as poetry now originates, not from the deep necessity that characterizes the work of a poet like Robinson Jeffers, but as a careerist venture, a professional marker, so to speak, and from which the author may proceed, if he or she is lucky, to a higher rung on the professional ladder. But that kind of success has little to do with the deep and lasting achievement in a genuine work of art.

The stately measure of Jeffers' lines is not merely a matter of verse technique, but a passionate conviction that energizes the verse lines and forms them into a pattern that will seem, to the alert reader, inevitable. And this is opposed to the non-verse of much contemporary writing: no substance, no conviction, just a form of self-amusement very much in tune with what has been called "the entertainment state."

And it is here that I would quote from the critical writing of Hayden Carruth, speaking of an older discipline now mostly set aside:

> You believe your writing can be a separate part of your life, but it can't. A writer's writing occurs in the midst of, and by means of, all the materials of life, not just a selected few. . . . And it isn't a paradox that you can choose necessity, if you seek the right objectives; and it will be no less inexorable because you have chosen it. Once you are in it, your writing will be in it also.
>
> (*Reluctantly*, p. 38)

It is here that the example of Robinson Jeffers makes a necessary appearance. He seems deliberately to have chosen his own necessity, as stonemason, builder, and poet, and to have made the most of it. The life and the work came together, the one nourishing the other.

In "Poets Without Prophecy," an essay written in 1963 and published in *The Nation,* Carruth had this to say of a contemporary shift in writing from substance to technique:

There was something grand and ennobling in the idea that a

poet was to be known not by his art but by his vision. . . . something essential. And we have lost it. . . .

Once the poet was our spokesman . . . and if he did not speak for all of us . . . if his poems lacked the larger vision of humanity, we said that he was deficient in one of the qualities that, by virtual definition, make a poet.

("Working Papers," pp. 54—55)

And he goes on to discuss some of the major figures in modern poetry who:

"came into the world at a time when the poet's direct responsibility to mankind at large hadn't been laughed out of existence. . . . This erosion of the larger view has reached a point at which poetry has become almost totally apolitical."

("Working Papers," p. 56)

I think that even a casual reading of contemporary poetry will verify the truth in that statement. And further (to quote again from Carruth): "the poet within himself identifies and augments the general experience in such a way that it will excite a renewed susceptibility in everyone else." He then goes on to quote the French poet Theophile Gautier: "To be of one's own time—nothing seems easier and nothing is more difficult."

It is true that this voice to which I refer, confirmed here by Carruth, can be heard at times in the work of other poets of our early modern period, and Jeffers was by no means alone, as different in their verse as most of them were. e. e. Cummings, for example, did not hesitate to excoriate his contemporaries, as in the following:

pity this busy monster manunkind
not. Progress is a comfortable disease,

31

your victim, life and death safely beyond,
plays with the littleness of his bigness.

And William Carlos Williams, as distant from Jeffers
in his style and thinking as he was, could write often in that
plainspoken voice of his, as in the darkness of wartime:

These
are the desolate dark weeks
when nature in its barrenness
equals the stupidity of man.

Or, in another and earlier poem, speaking of what he
refers to as "The Pure Products of America":

as if the earth under our feet
were
an excrement of some sky

and we degraded prisoners
destined
to hunger until we eat filth.

Who among our current generation of poets would speak
so directly to a potential audience? A fair question, one that
needs to be asked.

I think we can say that Jeffers is very much in that tradition,
the only tradition that really matters: that of the poet and artist
as speaker of the truth. The voice underlying the words has that
necessary continuity I associate with a kind of mastery. When
I think of what we can call the permanent work of our time,
Jeffers was, and is, of that company.

I don't mean to imply that a poet who falls outside this
tradition is to be dismissed as of no consequence. There are

many styles and modes, voices in poetry and song, that give pleasure and for one reason or another are deserving of praise. My major concern here has been with that other, public voice.

Edwin Muir concludes one of his lectures in his important book, *The Estate of Poetry*, with the following remarks:

> Our world presents the imagination with certain questions not asked before, or not asked in the same way. Public indifference [to poetry] may be expected to continue, but perhaps the audience will increase when poetry loses what obscurity is left in it by attempting greater themes, for great themes have to be clearly stated. A great theme greatly stated might still put poetry back in its old place.
>
> ("Poetry and the Poet", p. 93)

If that task is ever achieved, in our time or in the future of poetry, certainly Robinson Jeffers will be among those who made it possible.

Some Thoughts on Poetry and
the Call for Patriotism at This Time

In response to an invitation to offer a comment on Robinson Jeffers' poem, "The Purse-Seine," I was reminded of a brief article in a recent issue of the Hudson Review, in which the author, Michael Lind, voiced what appears to be a consistently negative opinion of poets who, like Jeffers, have undertaken in their verse a serious criticism of our national life and politics. According to Mr. Lind, our present is a time when our poets should give voice to a renewed patriotism, supportive of our president and his allies in Congress. It is in this debatable context that a poet like Jeffers stands clear as a representative figure, one now needed as perhaps never before.

The overall implications in Mr. Lind's piece seem to be that we should all, poets and citizens, rally around the flag at this threatened hour, and in one way or another condemn those who dare to question or refute the views and edicts of our present national administration given us under the protective label of "security."

The question then arises: Where would this assumed attitude have left those in the past who, like John Dryden, Alexander Pope, and Oliver Goldsmith, in their major poems ventured a serious criticism of some of the ruling political figures of their time, and of public behavior in general? To praise modern industrial society, its scope and products, as Mr. Lind would seem to have us do, is at best a simplification, and offers us little in the way of a needed reexamination of modern history and its consequences.

What we need, and what the art requires of us, is a serious critique of our manner of being, our ways of life and thought. And this is what a poet like Jeffers at his best offers us, whether or not we agree with all that he has to say. I would mention here also, essential as it is, the quality, the mastery, of the verse, its resonance and authority, permanently linked to the life and thought of the poet; that is, the two cannot be separated.

Our greatest poets, whether we speak of Dante, of Milton, Yeats, and Eliot, as well as many other prominent moderns like W. C. Williams, E. E. Cummings, and Jeffers, have been those who, in their very different styles, instinctively undertook a necessary appraisal of contemporary life in language resonant with what we continue to call "truth."

An irresponsible, one-sided criticism of American politics at this time will not serve as well; but neither will a misguided approval of those policies and the figures of authority behind them, all under the aegis of patriotism and national security. What we require of our poets, and reflection on recent events as they relate to the historical past and to a possible future, whether in this country, in Latin America, the Middle East, or elsewhere in what we refer to as the "Third World," the many people who continue to be severely affected by our policies. And with this, an ability to express these reflections in a memorable verse, one that our common reader can turn to and find in it a certain wisdom and a form of reconciliation.

This, it seems to me, is what Jeffers in "The Purse-Seine" attempted to do, and as in so many of his best poems succeeded in doing: a major reason why the poems survive and continue to instruct us.

2002

Post Haste, Post Everything

> What is *not* interesting is that which does not
> add to our knowledge of any kind; that which
> is vaguely conceived and loosely drawn.
> —Matthew Arnold

When this anthology arrived in the mail I was impressed at first with its thickness and weight, then by its title. *Postmodern American Poetry** would seem to cover a great deal of ground, an entire historical period, and might alone justify the heft of the volume, leaving room for poets of many sorts and persuasions. Aren't we all, I thought, in some way postmodern, if one understands by that the fact of coming after the first generation of moderns, whose achievement might, for some at least, seem so overwhelming as to constitute a major aesthetic barrier?

When I leafed through the anthology I found myself both surprised and disappointed. Where were the names I expected to find, and the poems? Where were Louis Simpson, James Wright, Donald Hall, and others of my generation? Where

---

**Postmodern American Poetry*, edited by Paul Hoover (New York: W.W. Norton, 1994)

were Wendell Berry, Thomas McGrath, and William Stafford? Where, given the context and the poetics, were older poets like George Oppen and Kenneth Rexroth?

And then it became clear to me that I was for the moment engaged with what appeared to be a subculture of poetry, whose prominent names included Charles Olson and Robert Duncan, Diane Wakowski and Ron Padgett, Anne Waldman and David Lehman, along with an array of younger talents, many of them previously unknown to me. A school, if you like—roughly dating from the early 1950s to the late 1980s—made up predominately of actors and declaimers, one of whose major premises seemed to be that the poem as traditionally understood and met with on the printed page, to be hand-carried in a book or committed to memory, had become obsolete, and what now mattered was the poem—or typographical arrangement of words and half words—intended for delivery to an audience, and essentially a performance art. And if that was so, then why so massive a collection of "poems" intended for the printed page, to be read and assessed as such?

Nonetheless, here it was, if only by its weight demanding attention and some estimate of its value to a potential reader. A typical example from this poetry, chosen more or less at random, might read like this:

> Ink of this Egyptian knock over night
> when the belly calms the whole roars, rows
> of anything inch to ape the dust, the ouncing
> Can you one-hand raise the Proper Vehicle?
> (Clark Coolidge, P. 375)

The two chief mentors behind this poetry would seem to be Ezra Pound and W. C. Williams, among the inventors of the age, and for many of us, initially at least, sources to be cherished even when not freely imitated. From their innovations in line and stanza, in their concept of the poem, has come much of the verse we wish to keep alive.

The anthology opens with Charles Olson, whose essay "Projective Verse" also opens the prose critical theory section of the book. Much of what follows in the anthology can be attributed to Olson and his ideas—ideas that in turn derive mainly from Pound and Williams, while Olson attempts a kind of codification of them for his own purposes. The confusion in Olson's arguments, the studied innovations in his verse style, can be traced throughout the anthology, and account for what is most at fault here: the formlessness, the posturing and self-promotion, the absence of a convincing intellectual structure, and much else of a negative cast. Here is a typical passage from Olson's essay:

> [A] poem is energy transferred from where the poet got it . . . by way of the poem itself to, all the way over to the reader. Okay. Then the poem itself must, at all points, be a high energy-construct and, at all points, an energy-discharge.
>
> ("Projective Verse, p. 614)

Having absorbed the mannerisms in Olson's prose, one may feel impelled to ask whether a Keats ode, or perhaps Arnold's "Dover Beach," is not of its nature a *high energy-construct,* as offensive as the pseudo technocratic formulation may be. But it is by way of such formulations that Olson gained the audience he sought and needed among younger poets at the time. A lengthy examination of Olson's arguments lies beyond the scope of this review, but undertaken in the right spirit would reveal, I believe, a surprising amount of phony scholarship.

The pretentiousness in Olson's prose is matched by a similar quality in his verse:

> The landscape (the landscape!) again: Gloucester,

the shore one of me is (duplicates), and from which
(from offshore, I, Maximus) am removed, observe.
("The Librarian," p. 15)

One observes here mainly the oddities in phrasing, the eccentric references to a fictional self, the straining after effect, and so forth which are easily duplicated in any number of examples from later poets in this anthology. For example, this from Charles Bernstein:

Who's on first? The dust descends as
the skylight caves in. The door
closes on a dream of default and
denunciation (go get those pizazzas),
hankering after frozen (prose) ambiance.
("Whose Language", p. 570)

And so on. Taken simply as fun, as play with language, such stuff may amuse for a page or two, but when confronted with close to six-hundred pages of it the un-indoctrinated reader might well wonder if a terminal disaster had struck the language, and we would soon be speaking gibberish to one another. This is, by and large, a poetry cut off from normal discourse and apparently content to speak to itself alone.

If, as Robert Creely says, quoted by Hoover in his introduction, "meaning is not importantly referential" (p. xxvii), then we are at a point of moral and aesthetic vacancy, and on the evidence of most of the work here, anything goes and nothing is of greater value than anything else.

As if to verify just how pervasive this thinking can be, here is a sample of poetic theory from Charles Bernstein:

My interest in not conceptualizing the field of the poem as a unitary plane, and so also not using overall structural programs:

that any prior principle of composition violates the priority I want to give to the inherence of surface, to the total necessity in the durational space of the poem.

You can write this way about poetry only if you believe that a poem is an object, subject to mechanical laws, of value to the extent that it obeys those laws. Let us contrast Bernstein's statement with a brief comment by Wendell Berry: "The form of a poem is invisible. A poem is not an 'object'. This is hard to accept in a mechanical age" ("Unspecializing Poetry").

A further indication of the attitude that underlies much of this anthology can be grasped in a comment by John Ashbery as quoted by Hoover: "Most reckless things are beautiful, just as religions are beautiful because of the strong possibility that they are founded on nothing" (p. xxxi). On the contrary. Religions, when alive, or even when in decay, are beautiful because they are founded on *something*, and on the certainty that this something governs all of life and human conduct. Without that something, human life tends radically to the chaos and civil disorder we find increasingly present among us today. And it is, by extension, precisely the order imposed on the random material of life by the creative intelligence that makes the difference in art and literature, and in philosophy as well.

One of the more irritating characteristics of the critical commentaries in this anthology is the recurring use of the word "organic" in reference to poetic form. Let it be said here that the form of a classical ode, in the hands of a Keats or a Wordsworth— or for that matter, the rhymed quatrain as adapted by Coleridge for his *Ancient Mariner*—becomes in fact *organic*, and does so mainly through its transformation by a true poet. The process is mysterious, but is related to the growth of things in the world at large. Certainly, the form of an Eliot "Quartet" becomes organic through that poet's use of it, his invention of it, based as it is on

40

past forms and usage. It is, in the end, the example in all of its mastery that makes the difference.

We can hardly hope to escape from the basic forms of the art and retain anything of that art. As sentence and paragraph are fundamental to prose, so line and stanza are basic to verse. Break these up as you will, into a visually interesting pattern on the page, the poem sooner or later returns to that which is of its nature, and without which it cannot exist. And I say this while acknowledging that poetry—in the larger, epic sense of it—can exist convincingly as prose—in the form of prose narrative, in the novel.

An additional problem with the work in this anthology is that it does not avoid the narcissism and sentimentality that Hoover in his introduction attributes to "the mainstream." If it is that "egotistical sublime" referred to here by Olson, that we are to be rid of, could there be anything more burdened and deformed by ego than the typical poem collected here?

> Our skin, strenuously tutored to appreciate
> the vernacular
> body a feeling might have. Companies
> of hands, legs, cigarettes, a whip, the sea . . .
> (Marjorie Welish, p. 444)

In writing like this, postmodernism is already a dead style. "Composition by field," as originally proposed by Olson, is a bogus theory. As if the working out of a canto by Dante did not constitute working in a "field"—a space in the mind, or the imagination— and for which the printed page is a form of testimony, a proof of permanence.

It has been tempting, while considering what to say of this volume, to simply quote from the poems and let these speak for themselves without commentary. But I would like at this point to make use of what I feel is a valid comparison. The following lines are quoted from a late poem by Wallace Stevens:

And a third form, she that says
Goodbye in the darkness, speaking quietly there,
To those that cannot say goodbye themselves.
("The Owl in the Sarcophagus")

And here are the opening lines of a poem by Ashbery:

The arctic honey blabbed over the report causing darkness
And pulling us out of there experiencing it
he meanwhile . . . And the fried bats they sell there
dropping from sticks . . .
("Leaving the Atocha Station" p. 170)

An even more extreme example from Susan Howe:

heroine in ass-skin
mouthing O Helpful
- father revivified waking when
nickname Hero men take pity   spittle   speak
("White Foolscap" p. 351)

It is saddening that the grace and command, the grave seriousness of a Stevens should have been reduced to the random catalogue of an Ashbery, to the declamatory nonsense of a Howe. And further, that so few are aware of the difference, of the transition and decline that are implied here. The various visual tricks by which the poems are ordered on the page cannot disguise the basic lack of substance in them. What little is being said, or that might be said, would require a concentration beyond the abilities of most of these poets, a fact of which they seem unaware. Poetry like this arises from a fundamental immaturity in the culture. Games, wordplay, snickers, nose-thumbing—a tabloid equivalent of the art; the equal in verse of a Warhol in painting, closer to a media event than an artistic one. For the most part, these poets fail for lack of what Williams in his best work demonstrably had: details, particulars, of the actual physical world around him, and of the human individuals who were present also. What we have here, typically, is the interior of minds not in themselves of great interest.

Having lived uncomfortably with this anthology for several months, my general impression is of a sprawling, untutored adolescence, apparently afflicted with a vast craving for attention. Toward the end of it, whether it is Tom Clark, Clark Coolidge, Robert Grenier, or Susan Howe, it all begins to sound the same, the product of people who do not know when to stop talking. Is there any essential difference between the running-off-at-the-mouth verse of, say, David Antin, and the general aspect of the mass media? I doubt it. There are few poems here that could not have been substantially improved by revision. Much that might have been made into something worthwhile is simply thrown away.

This description is admittedly unfair to the few good poets and worthwhile poems contained herein. With careful selection, from Levertov, Ferlinghetti, Snyder, Ginsberg, and so forth along with a handful of things from a few of the later poets, a modest addition to our poetry might have been made. Robert Duncan had a voice and style of his own, and there are moments of coherence and beauty in his work. In a major poem printed here, "A Poem Beginning with a Line by Pindar," a brief passage of seventeen lines naming some of the American presidents might well stand on its own as a poem. Gregory Corso's "Marriage" remains for some a classic. Russell Edson's "Ape" is a poem among the best of its kind, but in its inventive humor not easily repeated. The first stanza of John Wieners' "'The Waning of the Harvest Moon" is striking in its momentary seriousness. As for Allen Ginsberg, represented here by a few pages from "Howl" and selections from two or three later poems, and though I have always been taken with his meeting Walt Whitman in a supermarket, I am often reminded of a remark by Louis Simpson many years ago, that the opening lines of "Howl," in which Ginsberg claims to have seen "the best minds" of his generation, are untrue; he saw nothing of the sort.

Paul Hoover's introduction, even where one disagrees with much of what he proposes, is probably as inclusive a discussion of the scene as one could expect, given the scope of this book and the number of writers included. Yet even the best among these poets, and they are mostly the older ones, seem in the context oddly weightless, not sufficiently represented by their best work. In fairness, it would be difficult to imagine any poet, on the basis of a brief selection in an anthology like this one, not being submerged in the mass of mediocrity so much in evidence here.

This is not the only oversized collection of poetry in this vein. While completing this review I happened on a copy of *From the Other Side of the Century: A New American Poetry.* Even larger and heavier than the present collection, it has the minor advantage that a few older poets of the school—Louis Zukowski, Charles Reznikov, and George Oppen, among them—are represented. The same general foolishness, however, abounds from page to page.

We have here roughly six-hundred pages of poems and biographical notes, with an additional seventy or so pages of critical theory. There have been moments in my consideration of this volume when in desperation I would have sought out a copy of Fitzgerald's *Omar Khayyam* to reassure myself that poetry, in the old and durable sense, still mattered. I feel confident in saying that I would trade this entire anthology for Wordsworth's "The Simplon Pass," for Edward Thomas's "The Coomb" for Yeats's "The Song of the wandering Aengus," for a page or two of Edwin Muir or Thomas Hardy. My best hope is that another generation of poets might be brought to see the folly of a school of poetics as represented here, resolve to grow up, and move on to better things.

The problem for poetry now remains what it has been: to absorb the lessons of modernism and, while retaining the best tradition, to make of that example something new, while never forgetting the substance of a remark by Stevens: that it is not the form as such, but what is created in the poem itself that finally matters. And to that one might usefully add the following from Edwin Muir: "There remains the temptation for poets to turn inward into poetry, to lock themselves into a hygienic prison where they speak only to one another ("The Estate of Poetry"). Muir's warning finds in this anthology ample proof of its truth, and one would have to say the same for most poetic criticism now being written.

1994-1995

Not Yet Angels

A major anthology of new formalist poets may present the uninitiated reader/reviewer with some difficulty. He must identify what it is the editors and poets are attempting to do, decide if it is worth doing, and, finally, determine how well they succeed in doing it.

Direct comparisons of examples of writing can often be useful. Here is a free verse stanza taken at random from a recent issue of *Ohio Review.*

> Here is what evening tells us mathematically:
> the probability of morning
> is commensurate. We take to pacing,
> hastening back and forth
> embodying recognition just this one way.

And here is the concluding stanza from a poem by one of the editors of this anthology, David Mason.

> Tonight the temperature is due to fall,
> an arctic stillness settles on the prairies. . .
> The years slow down and look about for shelter

far from forests and far from summer ponds:
the mind ghosting out in a shoal of stars.

Read aloud, the first example appears to be nothing more than lined out prose, flat in its cadence, and without distinction of any kind. In Mason's unrhymed pentameter, the cadence is quiet and effective in its regularity. Two poles of the argument, if you will, neither of them extreme.

The new formalist movement has been with us for some time, and a number of books, both prose and verse, have appeared in recent years in support of a return to metrical verse and the neglected forms of traditional poetry. *Rebel Angels* is a substantial contribution to the discussion. It has received generally favorable reviews, and in fact there is much to commend here in the work of Dana Gioia, Marilyn Hacker, Charles Martin, and R. S. Gwynn, among others.

I have recorded elsewhere my views regarding some of the claims for achievement in this movement.* It is not, for example, a "revolution." A revival, yes; a renewal, if you like, or perhaps a restoration. Nor were those who wrote formal verse in the postmodern period "suppressed," as the editors would have it in their otherwise useful introduction. The presence of terms like these, the revolutionary fervor that seems to motivate them, impresses me as more of a promotional device than an accurate assessment of the condition of poetry in recent decades.

It is easy to point to the prosaic monotony of much contemporary free verse, but the monotony of rhymed iambics so much in evidence here offers but slight improvement. Rhyme, I think, should surprise us, not merely soothe us and remind us of echoes from the past when rhyming was a predictable and necessary part of the music of verse. And one problem I have with many of these poems is that there is seldom a surprise in them.

Above the baby powder clouds
The sky is china blue.
Soon, young and chattering, the crowds
Of stars come pushing through.
    (Frederick Turner, "Spring Evening")

Thus, even in Dryden's day it was possible to complain of the "dull sweets of rhyme."

Otherwise, there is nothing inherently wrong with celebrating odd moments of our common domestic and personal life; much of the inheritance of poetry is made of such moments. Nonetheless, the better part of the work collected here leaves me with the feeling of a number of gifted people in search of something to write about. For what these poets lack is just that intimation of a larger theme, that which lies beyond the ordinary time and place. It is possible to see in the work of many of these poets confirmation of the self-consoled isolation of Americans in a world of immense suffering, aggravated, often enough, by our own extravagance.

As for the argument, free versus formal, I believe that the best poetry of our time will continue to make use of the potential in both free and formal measures. In this respect, it is useful to recall Eliot's remark as to the "ghost of a meter" he felt should underlie even the freest of free verse. Nor should we discount the insight in another remark by Eliot, that the innovations of the early modernists were "a step in making the modern world possible in art." Certainly Eliot and his contemporaries succeeded in that.

There are, to be sure, some fine and worthwhile poems here. Dana Gioia's dramatic narrative "Counting the Children" has been justly praised. Marilyn Hacker's late lament for James Wright is among the more moving pieces to be found here. I would mention also Mary Jo Salter's engaging "Frost at Midnight," and Charles Martin's "Easter Sunday, 1985," one poem that takes on a contemporary political subject and does so effectively. I have returned also to Bruce Bawer's sonnet on looking down from an aircraft at night, and to its central question:

> Would even Wordsworth, seeing what I see,
> know that these lights are not well-ordered stars
> that have been here a near-eternity,
> but houses, streetlamps, factories, and cars?

Consideration of this volume suggests far more than another skirmish between the free verse school and a resurgent formalism, and a good deal more than can be adequately dealt with in a brief review. There is the persistent question of an audience. Earlier generations of poets could still assume, and as a matter of cultural inheritance, that they spoke, if only potentially, to an audience in society at large. Indeed, one can hardly imagine a poet like Robinson Jeffers writing under any other condition; and Yeats, as we know, claimed that as a poet he could not write without his audience. In contrast, poets now seem to be speaking mainly to themselves in a world where few others are listening.

Finally, then, it is the direction in which a collection like this may lead that is of concern here. One of our prominent formalists remarked in a letter to me last year that he did not care if his poems had any social or political content. Fair enough, as far as it goes, but history, I think, will care.

It can be fairly suggested, and in keeping with the basic argument underlying this anthology, that at this time the emphasis for the serious and innovative poet must be on craft and reclaiming for poetry something of what has been lost with the abandonment of traditional metrics in the postmodern period. And when that is accomplished, the poets may be willing to take a wider subject matter, and speak freely on public issues as well as on private passions. Perhaps, I remain skeptical that the prevailing disposition in these poets will allow that to happen.

The one thing that might alter the present state of mind is the energy of events in the outside world—in the social and political sphere—and which might in turn release a responding energy in the poets, changing the language and its usage as it does so. This is what took place in the early modern period, and continues to be a force among poets elsewhere in the world.

In the end, it is always content that determines the permanence of a work of art. Not technique as such, though that may often be of interest, but craft in the service of that something larger, as Stevens, among other poets in our time, understood very well. The true form lies within the poem, in what is being said there, and for which the chosen verse form is a sign of discipline.

Anyone concerned with contemporary poetry will find this anthology of more than casual interest. Read along with a dictionary of poetic terms, it may appear as a worthwhile if limited guide. The concluding pages offer an index to the forms used throughout.

The poetry, however, is another matter. It may be instructive at this point to offer one more brief comparison. Here are the opening lines of a poem by Timothy Steele, one of the prominent names among the "rebels."

> Emerging through the automatic doors
> I feel the Santa Ana's gusting heat.
> It's five o'clock. The grainy sunlight pours
> Through eucalypti whose peeled bark strips beat
> The trunks to which they cling like feeble sleeves.
>   ("The Library")

And here are the final stanzas from W. H. Auden's poem for the German poet Ernst Toller, who died in New York in 1939.

We are lived by powers we pretend to understand:
They arrange our loves, it is they who direct
    at the end
The enemy bullet, the sickness, or even our hand.

It is their tomorrow hangs over the earth of the living
And all that we wish for our friends: but existence
    is believing
We know for whom we mourn and who is grieving.

The metrical command is Auden's verse can hardly be questioned, but there is something else present when compared with examples from our representative formalists, and which sets the work in another dimension altogether: that instinctive grasp of the essential content of one's time, together with the intuition that history does matter, and the poet cannot escape it.

In these lines, measured and moving, Auden touches on a theme far beyond his personal situation or passing mood, and speaks for a generation, an epoch, a way of life and thought.

And with these thoughts in mind, let the reader decide.

1997

The Story of a Poem

We have been building it
for thousands of years,
this emptiness where grief
is blowing, a gust
from a frozen fountain.

Where a man, primitive,
with a cluster of stars
at his shoulder,
moves intently into a deepening
twilight of the ego –

the poem becoming Night.

(1964)

The story of this poem is largely one of accretion, of an intermittently conscious search for the key to its possible development from the early version of it reprinted here. The following incidents and details in one way or another contributed to the poem and may be of some interest.

A postcard photo of the Horse Nebula, and some random study

of the better known constellations, the winter figure of Orion being among the most important.

Another postcard photo of a limestone sculpture from an old church in southern France. The card was sent to me by W. S. Merwin sometime in the late 1960s, and showed St. Luke seated with a book open on his knees, with the head of an ox emerging from the stone and facing him as if listening to whatever it was the saint might be reading.

A quotation from the sixteenth century Spanish poet Luis de Gongora. I have forgotten just where in Gongor's poetry I found the phrase.

Some lines from Canto XXVI of the <u>Inferno</u>, in which Ulysses urges his men toward a destiny beyond the sun in a world without humanity.

Exactly how these elements were to fit into the scheme of the poem and in what sequence I would find difficult to verify other than for the evidence that shows up in the various drafts I have kept with me over the years. I seem to recall working on the poem while living in England in 1977, and thereafter at intervals when I returned to this country. But it has only been within the past year or so that I returned to the poem with the intention of finishing it.

As important as anything to the *thought* in the poem is the intuition that we citizens of this planet may be passing into a new phase of existence, whether for good or ill we cannot know, and which carries with it the possibility of a world devoid of spiritual meaning as we have known it in the past, with the ancient symbols cast into doubt and the constellations merely numbers in a void. I would add to this the thought that beyond the earth imagery of traditional poetry we may have need of new, or farther, field of imagination.

Finally, a form, a verse structure, that would satisfy me as being consistent with whatever meaning the poem may have. Perhaps here too Dante has been a guide.

1992

A Poem Without Meaning

The spittle of the silent stars . . .
—Gongora

We have been building it for
thousands of years, this emptiness
where grief is blowing,

a gust from a frozen fountain.
History is now undone, on a field
where red giants and white

dwarfs oppose each other, clash
and bestride the dust.
An immense horse grazes there,

trailing a thread of spittle.
He draws no chariot,
he runs no race, riderless

in the great cloud of himself.
Through a forest of electric trees
comes now an alien force –

a wind off the farthest glacier,
the haunt of huge auguries,
arms whirling, catching at space.

Remember now, St. Luke and the Ox:
how the mute and docile creature
kneeled to be instructed . . .

And as the saint was reading, intent
on his fabulous words, the page
before him burned to a black hole.

There are no more ballads, wiry
and pitched to the stars;
no aerial stages, no strutting boards.

No stretched and glittering figures
with the names of heroes,
heroes with the names of men . . .

All speeches of pith and grandeur
put away with weights and measures
in the deep mind of God.

Words spoken in the winter of Mars,
in the dusk of Saturn,
compose themselves . . .

The poem becoming Night.

(1964–1992)

III

ALASKA:
STORIES & REVIEWS

A Night on Cabin Creek

All of my hunting experience during my homestead years, the 1950s and 1960s, left me with a very deep and enduring impression. I was never a sport hunter, and had I not during that early period put myself into a way of life that required a singular attention to the basic needs that would allow me the means to continue that life, and especially when adequate financial means were not available, it is unlikely that I would have been able to remain on that remote plot of land overlooking the Tanana River and make of it the life I had only dreamed of when I first settled there as a postwar homesteader in the late 1940s.

I have written little of my specific hunting experience: the tracking and calling, the killing of the moose, and then the labor of butchering the carcass and saving those essential parts that would make it possible to survive another long winter and keep us fed, with the vegetable crop in storage, and the salmon harvest that was smoked and dried, stored in a cold cellar and sometimes canned; but it was the moose that closed that long season of labor with the assurance that we had what we needed to survive.

There is much I might write of those moose-hunting years, shared with my companion, Jo, who had joined me in the late 1950s, but I will tell here the story of one moose hunt, how it happened and why I have remembered it so clearly.

In August 1959 I had begun building a small cabin on a hillside overlooking a creek to which I had given the name Cabin Creek. Among the many creeks and tributaries of that Salcha River drainage, it was the only one that had no name on the maps. It was close to ten miles north of my homestead at Richardson in an isolated area long left behind when the gold rush years had faded. I had for some time thought of establishing a campsite that would give us a place that might serve as a hunting and trapping camp far from the highways and road traffic that fronted our main home cabin and yard. And here, after much thought and searching the many creeks and headwaters, the ridges and domes in the area, I had finally found the right place.

After a summer of thought and planning, a search for the needed materials, I had set up a campsite for us on the small bluff above the creek and close to the spot of land I had chosen for the cabin. I had put up a wall tent large enough for the two of us to sleep in, and with a small sheet-iron stove into which I could feed the wood scraps saved from the cabin work and which would keep us warm in the fall, which was now on its way, and would also allow the cooking of a meal when it was needed. A kerosene lantern, and a flashlight, would make it possible to keep track of things in the building work as the fall sunlight faded behind the hills to the south.

Remote as it was, the cabin work went slowly in the time I could spare from the fall homestead chores that also required my labor and presence. We needed something here on Cabin Creek that would allow us permanent shelter in the distance from home and in the months and seasons to come. The log walls were slowly taking shape, having laid the foundations and a temporary flooring. With the month of September already upon us, I looked forward to having the roofing in place, and then the indoors work, with a couple of windows and a good sturdy door. It would take time, and the cabin would not be fully finished and furnished until the following summer. Meanwhile, the tent was our shelter.

And soon enough, with the cabin work occupying much of my time, came the moose season, one of the major events of our life, always uncertain as to when and where I might find that animal that would keep us through the winter now on its way. I felt certain that in the creeks and swamps, the densely wooded slopes, there were a few moose, and in their tracks and other signs I could read what I needed to know when the time came: that a bull moose, perhaps the right one, was close and would soon be active in the rutting season now on its way.

In that fall season, with the bull moose in search of a mating cow, it was possible, with the skill and acquired knowledge, to imitate a bull by voice or with the right piece of antler or simply a dry stick to be rubbed or thrashed in the brush, and to call one close enough to be killed. I had learned this, how best to do it, from an old Richardson neighbor, and I found that with some skill and practice, at the right time, in the right place, it might work.

We were sleeping in the tent one night, having gone to bed early after a long day of work at the cabin site. We had left the dogs at home, but Jo would return to feed them the following day while I stayed on to continue the cabin work.

With the possibility of a moose somewhere close by, perhaps attracted by the sound of my cabin woodwork before I went into the tent for the night, I spent some brief time rubbing a section of moose antler on one of the nearby willows. In the stillness and quiet that prevailed around our campsite, I also called by voice with the aid of my carefully rolled tube of birth bark, a tool I had learned to use that would concentrate the sound of my grunting and occasional moan aimed toward the quiet woods that surrounded our camp. And then, having placed my tools aside, I spent a few quiet moments listening into the dusk that was slowly coming into the well-treed hollow where we were camped. But I heard nothing in the stillness that surrounded us. The evening sky was clear, and we expected some moonlight in the fall night that was coming.

Sometime after going to bed, rolled in a heavy sleeping bag that was part of our camp, I was awakened by a sound that came to me thought the tent wall: a rustling of leaves and branches, and then what sounded like the cracking of a small tree branch. I knew at that moment that there was a moose close by in the woods not far from our camp. I put aside the sleeping robe, got quietly to my feet and found my god hunting rifle where I had placed it close to the bed. With no more than a pair of heavy socks on my feet, I quietly opened the tent flap and went out into the night, to stand there with my rifle in hand, listening. Jo was still asleep in the tent, and I did not want to wake her.

I found my section of moose antler where I had placed it close to the tent, and I quietly rubbed it against a branch of one of the willows that stood near the tent. I heard nothing in reply. And then, after a few minutes of waiting for a response, I let my rifle rest against a tree trunk, and with my hands cupped about my mouth and lips, in the voice I had learned and practiced many times, I called to the moose with a low grunting I knew might arouse that hidden bull still somewhere out there in the nearby woods. Then I stood still and waited, listening for any sound that might come from that other being out there.

Soon enough I heard the moose thrashing his horns in the nearby brush. I could not see him, but I knew he was close. With my hands once more cupped about my mouth, I called him again. In the quiet that followed I heard the bull moose breathing. And then, with what sounded like a deep sigh, he moved away, and I heard nothing more. I was left standing there in a silence I knew might not be broken again.

After standing there in the quiet, with the moonlight overhead in the trees, and beginning to feel the night frost in my feet and hands, I went quietly back into the tent. I laid my rifle aside, and lay down again under the sleeping robe, and soon went back to sleep, half dreaming of what I had experienced in those brief and quiet moments. It was not until the next morning that I told Jo what had happened. She had been only briefly aware that I had gotten up and left the tent, and then she had gone back to sleep.

It was perhaps a week later that I was at work on the cabin roof, fitting poles and boards to contain the heavy damp moss which I had planned to serve as insulation for the coming winter. Fall was now with us, with a deep frost at night and a light dusting of snow on the ground. The moose rut was fully active, but I had not yet seen a bull I might claim and kill and which would keep us through the coming winter.

Occupied with some minor detail on the cabin roof, driving a nail, fitting a plank, I looked up from my work and glanced down into the flat below the cabin site, and saw to my sudden surprise a large bull moose feeding quietly along the small creek that was now slowly freezing. It was, I felt certain, the same moose that had responded to my calling and had come close to our tent that night I remembered so well. As I looked, the moose stopped feeding and looked up at the cabin site. To waste no time, I climbed down from the roof and found my rifle where I had left it in close reach. I steadied myself against a corner log of the cabin, and with the rifle at my shoulder, took careful aim at the moose where it stood below me with its broad flank so clear to my sight, and fired one shot at its neck. The moose started suddenly, took a few steps as if to run away, and then with a heavy sound I could hear and feel, it fell on its side. With a brief jerking of its limbs, it then lay still. The one shot and careful aim had done it.

A quiet moment followed, and then Jo was with me,

having heard the rifle shot on her way to the camp, hiking the trail from the homestead ridge. She stood beside me, quietly impressed by the kill we had hoped for.

With the moose now dead before us, we gathered axe and knife and climbed down into the creek bottom to where the moose lay without a sound or twitching of its limbs. As always, to approach the dead animal and realize what I had done in killing it was a sobering moment. As much as we needed that winter meat, I never felt any pleasure or sense of triumph in having killed so large and impressive a creature. But there it was. We went to work, turning the heavy carcass onto its back, and with knife and small axe I proceeded to cut it open, splitting the rib cage in half, and then removing the entrails, the heart, the liver and kidneys, any and all parts we might save for a future meal.

When I had cut the moose into its four separate quarters, removing its head with the antlers, which I planned to save and make some use of, I cut down four or five small trees growing nearby, whether birch or aspen. I trimmed them of branches and laid them on the wet and mossy ground in a compact group. One front quarter was set aside, to be cut into suitable pieces and taken home. We then tugged the remaining three quarters onto the group of poles, letting them lie close together. From a few spruce trees growing nearby I cut limbs and branches, enough to cover the moose quarters and, as I had planned and hoped, keep them safe and dry until I was able to hang them on a rack I had yet to build.

We dragged the one front quarter uphill to the cabin site where I went to work, cutting the ribs into pieces that might be packed away to the homestead many miles distant.

Within a short time, a day or two, having returned once more form the home cabin, I built a sturdy rack between two large spruce trees close to the cabin site where the remaining moose quarters would be hung and kept safe until, with sled and dogs and sufficient snow on the trail, I could bring them home for the winter. The hunt was over. The fall season was on us, and once more an essential part of that older subsistence life had been realized.

In a poem I wrote sometime later, and which I titled "Horns," the story is told in a more condensed form then I have written here. To live as we did then, and as many have in our now uncommon past, served to place one in a relation to nature and the indwelling elements of nature—the animals, the birds, the surrounding wilderness, and the ever changing weather of the seasons—all that related us to that older history we sometimes feel we have left behind in our civilized growth; but it is there, and will remain for those who, if only for a brief moment, take leave of our present modernization and return to that older, still potential life.

In the sudden stillness that followed on my calling of the moose, to stand and listen in the shadowy darkness that prevailed, I felt myself returned, however briefly, to a much older life when men and animals might speak to each other in a voice that was shared—with birds and insects also, but particularly with the animals that were hunted for food and who shared some part of the earth with us, and to whom we might speak when needed. In that still remembered moment I felt myself part of a life in which the elements, the weather patterns, the land itself in its many changing forms—the stars and planet formations to which we have given names, and as we can still see them, if only at night, in darkness, and indeed the sun itself—became part of an ancient drama, a story that will and must be told many times, and in certain essential respects, believed.

2008

Readings from an Alaskan Journal

Why write? Why tell stories and construct poems? Why labor over words and their meanings? Why struggle with thoughts, and with those elusive feelings, like fish falling through a net too large? Self-expression, in the most obvious and playful sense of this? Or is it something a few of us learn to do, and which happens to attract some attention in the world at large and, if we are lucky, may provide a living? It may be a little of all of these, but I think the most genuine justification for writing, for creating what we call literature, lies in this: that we are always, as writers and as individuals, under the obligation to give some account of ourselves and the world we have known, and that this activity remains one of the few ways we have of continuing ourselves in some truth and life in common.

Wendell Berry wrote something once I would like to quote: "we are dependent for understanding, and for consolation and hope upon what we learn of ourselves from songs and stories. This has always been so, and it will not change."

It is, in other words, a serious matter, and not to be taken lightly. I have always tried to approach my own life experience with some sense of this responsibility. It has not been easy. I was not born to any secure place, knowing from childhood where I belonged, geographically and culturally. I have never been able to claim identification with an ethnic group nor, except for my early years in Richardson, Alaska, with any closely bound community otherwise. Like most of us, I am the descendant of European immigrants, hardly yet at home on this continent. But I have nonetheless been trying all my life to understand the ground I walk on, and as a writer to tell as well as I can what I have found, what I think I know. All I have is this one imperfect and unfinished life, with the things, events, and persons that have in one way or another found a place in it, and who therefore have some claim upon it. I must do my best by them, believing that if what I have seen and felt has any truth in it, that truth, or sense of life, will have meaning for others.

Over a dozen years ago I published a slim book of poems that embodied the essence of my experience in Alaska to that time. Ruminating on those years in the meantime, I have realized that there is a great deal more to the story, and that the story ought to be told. I became aware of the extent to which I had for years listened to the old people at Richardson and had stored away in my mind everything they told me, and had recorded so many details of the life and place that when I tried to write about it, I hardly knew where to begin. But I had to begin somewhere, and as is often the case, the best place to begin is somewhere in the middle of it. So I have gone back over the thirty some years I have known Alaska—farther back than that, in fact, to the beginnings of my own youthful interest in the North, to my readings in the many books and stories written by others—and begun to compose this memory into some kind of narrative. In doing this, I have not only rediscovered the place and its resident people, but I have come to know new ground in myself.

I like the old things and ways; the older I get, the better I like them. I resist their displacement in myself, as well as their destruction in the world outside me. We hear it said of someone that he or she is "living in the past." This is taken to be a negative comment whenever applied. Personally, I see nothing wrong with living in the past; it is a perfectly good place to live. At the same time, I have to say that the demarcation seems to me to be false. It may be that only among such a perpetually transient and unsettled people as we North Americans have become, that this division of life into past, present, and future could have become so accepted and pernicious in our thinking. So, in the name of some impossible "progress" we habitually demolish the landmarks and replace them with an ever shoddier present. Meanwhile, as with so much else in contemporary life, we have long since assigned the "past" to specialists—to historians and archaeologists, souvenir hunters and antique dealers of one sort or another.

I believe it has not always been this way. In my mind, it ought not to be. The *right* place to live is a place in which past and present flow as a single experience, and together they make up the only future we are likely to have, the only sane and decent one.

Perhaps what all of this comes down to is *residence,* in the truest and deepest sense. What does it mean to be here. What clues can we find in the soil around us to the life that has been, is now, and may be tomorrow? Here in Alaska, as well as elsewhere, we can see how difficult is that needed residence, and the harm that continual change and uprooting inflicts on a land and its people. I know it all too well myself. Having lived and worked in many other places in recent years, I find myself drawn back in one way or another to the only ground I really know, in a kind of gentle bondage.

So I return to that obligation I spoke of at the beginning. For me, the writing is another phase of the life lived. Properly speaking, there would be no discontinuity, but ideally and at last, a reconciliation.

And finally, as for the significance of all this, perhaps it is a little like something an old, blind Irish storyteller said once to a woman tourist who asked him the age of some weathered and ciphered stones by the roadside in rural Ireland. And he replied: "Madam, we are much too young to know."

Foreword to *The Last New Land*

A couple of years ago, a woman acquaintance, a doctor in Fairbanks, remarked when I told her I might be moving to Anchorage: "For me, Anchorage is *not* Alaska." I knew what she meant by this; it was an expression I had heard from others in reference to the drastic imposition of a modern urban profile—of expressways and office high rises, of a bustling legal and commercial center—on a landscape still fundamentally new and uncultivated. Yet I replied to her: "But Anchorage *is* Alaska," a comment that caused her to reflect and say, "Well, you're right about that."

It is this divided response that characterizes the typical American attitude toward Alaska—a place physically remote to the majority of people yet immediate in its emotional appeal and dreamlike significance. No matter how familiar that repeated phrase "the last frontier," it remains true of Alaska in many ways, and represents a theme that requires continual evaluation as this century nears its end and the global state of mind now asserts itself, whether we mean by that the corporate exploitation of remaining resources or the more considerate response we know as environmental protection—the extremes within which the fate of lands and nations seems destined to be decided in our time.

There are, it seems to me, two latent and opposing forces at work in the settlement of a new land—opposing motives and consequences that, once set in motion, must play themselves out. Accordingly, the European colonization of North America has left in its wake much irresolution, and the arguments are still with us. To the thoughtful reader a collection of writings such as this [*The Last New Land*] presents these conflicting views: on the one hand, discovery and exploration, adventure and romance; and on the other, displacement and theft—all at one time accepted as "Manifest destiny."

We may otherwise think of this anthology as a guide: from an earlier intuitive and spiritual connection of land and people, in which an essential and precarious balance is maintained between the two, to the intrusion of an alien, competitive culture determined to seize both land and resources and wring from them the utmost in material profit. At this point in history, and despite the painted images and stirring written accounts, it is difficult to see anything admirable, for example, in the Russian encounter with the Natives of south coastal Alaska; and when the first flush of adventure is dispensed with, not much better can be said for the later incursions of American missionaries, gold seekers and fur traders. In nearly all instances the effect on native cultures was catastrophic.

In responding to what we read in this anthology, we may be excited, even enlightened, by the adventures, the romance and the poetry, and at times the deeper reflection that emerges. But we should also be awake to the instruction that is here for us in that repeated encounter of people with other peoples, aware now as we must be of the risks and abuses, the thoughtlessness and ruthlessness, of so many early encounters.

I write as one who, at an early age, felt that urge toward adventure in a new land, and who, rather than daydream about it, went to Alaska and lived out the potential in that dream. Having done that, it remained for me to think my experience through and write about it so that others might know something of what I had learned.

It is reasonable to ask, in view of our present diminished world, what is a young person today to dream on? What farther field of adventure, what new land or new people? What Africa, what Greenland or Alaska? On this planet we are running out of adventures in the old fashioned sense, losing those remote, mysterious places where something essential to our depleted modern sensibilities is still intact. Alaska is one of those places, though the attraction now would seem in part to be an illusion.

There have been moments when I wished we could leave some things and places alone. Once the grand features of Alaska, the high and noble peaks and remote hinterlands, were places of contemplation and veneration, the abode of the gods and the earth spirits, and beyond trespass. Our modern response is all too often the recreational equivalent of that will to dominate, to possess and exploit, every known resource and feature of the earth. And when those open, mysterious places can no longer be found, we may face a real and profound crisis; how we deal with this may be part of the true drama of the next century.

There is, then, a difference between the earlier writing to be found here, when a certain innocence prevailed, and later writing that reflects a time when that innocence is no longer possible. There is what we know as factual truth—of names, dates, and verifiable events: It is called history. And there is the truth of poetry, of myth and legend, which is in some ways more real than the truth of history, going deeper into the heart and meaning of things and events.

It is fitting, therefore, that the opening sections begin with Native legends and stories; in their essential poetry we are as close to the origin of things as we may get. The singularity of these stories is due to their grounding in myth and legend—in the suppositional text of nature from which all mystery and poetry ultimately derive. The factual reporting of events that is characteristic of our time can rarely compete with this. Myth and legend, converted to history, may again be reconciled in poetry, a way of speech and thought, of imagination, that can grasp the facts and return them to legend.

The range of material collected here is impressive. We find many of the familiar classics of the north, and numerous additions from more recent writing. It is especially rewarding to read the contributions of contemporaries like Tom Sexton, Linda Schandelmeir, Nick Jans, and Sheila Nickerson, among others. It is good also to enjoy once again a poem by Hamlin Garland, a nearly forgotten figure from an earlier day when poetry was still read and listened to by the general public. We may wonder what additional undiscovered material is out there by writers on Alaska few have heard of. What of the unpublished journals and letters that may survive the camps, the trails, and the temporary settlements? Someday an anthology might be made of these.

And another book could be collected of work by contemporary writers who have focused with clarity and passion on the social and political implications of our frontier exploitation of lands and peoples—the relentless efforts toward "development" that will not cease until the last resource is taken, the last fish caught, the last tree cut. The American rallying cry, as voiced once by Carl Sandburg, "Where to? What next?" will not be sufficient now.

So let us turn to this anthology and to the several versions of Alaska that live in the contemporary imagination. Among the dominant themes are those influenced by history and mythology, by geology and anthropology, and by a popular inclination to romance and poetry. All of these in some way refer back to the manifold history of this continent, a history that is, in many human respects, still to be realized. The reader will find here something of all of these, an imperfect and continuing record, as we near the end of the century. And something more: a celebration, of a land and its impact on the people who have come to live here, or who have ventured, if only for a brief time, into its hidden places.

1996

The Book of the Tongass
(Review)

Not many readers, I suspect, will be fully familiar with the subject of this book, the Tongass National Forest of southeast Alaska, a vast region of islands and coastal fiord lands stretching more than a thousand miles from Vancouver Island north to Prince William Sound. As briefly described here by Paul Alaback, one of the contributors to the book, "The Tongass forms the heart of the world's largest temperate rain forest."

*The Book of the Tongass** is a collection of writings by foresters, mill workers, biologists , fishermen, scholars, and storytellers, individuals whose lives have in some way been marked by the grandeur and relative remoteness of the Tongass. There are fourteen individual contributions to the collection, including two English- language versions of Tlingit tales of origins and Native life. The better part of these are concerned with the history of the region, its cultures, and, notably, the ongoing difficulties with the timber industry that has long sustained many of the island communities. At its best, the book offers a thorough study of a special part of our world, its

---

*Carolyn Servid and Donald Snow, ed. The Book of the Tongass (Minneapolis: Milkweed Editions, 1999).

capacities, its losses, what it has meant and should mean to the people who live there.

One does not necessarily agree with all that is written here. Donald Snow's assertion at the opening of his introduction, and referring to the oldest trees of the forest, now largely destroyed by the woodcutters, that "we shall never see them again," is affirmative in its way, but we know, some of us at any rate, that if our industrial civilization was removed from this earth, Nature will reassert itself. *We* may not see them, or it, again, but that does not mean that they, or it, will not return, to thrive and be seen again, perhaps, by another race of people.

Otherwise, Snow's introduction is reasoned and fair, the enthusiastic impression of someone come from the outside, to look and evaluate. As well as providing a useful outline of the book's content and purpose, he gives us in an honest fashion his impressions of the birds and animals doing what humanity does on a more destructive scale: making use of what is there, killing and cutting, living literally off the land, but in balance with that which can be replaced and is replaced in due time.

As might be expected, the emphasis in much of the writing is on timber: the forest, the trees, that which makes the region what it uniquely is. In John Sisk's "Logging and Learning in the Tongass Forest" we are given a history of logging in southeast Alaska, an informed discussion of the prospects for the timber industry, in the course of which Sisk asks the essential question: "how much can we take from the forest, how much can we enjoy the forest, without diminishing its capacity to provide?"

In Daniel Henry's "Allowable Cut: Fear and Transformation in a Tongass Timber Town" we have one town's (Haines, Alaska) problems with the mills and timber harvesting, the sometimes ugly confrontations between timber rights and environmentalists. What emerges from Henry's story is the insatiable appetite for profits, whether from timber, from gold or copper, a hunger that if unchecked will exhaust every resource and leave a given region to survive on remorse and destitution.

Tim Bristol's contribution, "The Independents: Hope All Over," gives us a look at the Tongass timber industry from the point of view of an independent operator in contrast to a dominating corporation like Ketchikan Pulp; of small-scale timbering and wood products, the gains and losses. The Smith and White family operations as introduced here by Bristol are a source of optimism. On another closely related issue, Brad Matson's account of the salmon fishery and the history of watersheds is excellent, among the better essays in the book. It is spirited and alive with its subject. Stewart Allen, in his "Forest Management: You Can't Stand Still," explores the logging options that remain with the closing of major corporations like Ketchikan Pulp, including in one instance the use of helicopters in selective logging. We are oddly introduced to programs with names like "ecosystem inventories," "science management," and to "research based" partnerships with the logging industry.

When I first read through the unpublished pages of this collection earlier this year, the contribution that in many respects struck me most forcibly was David Voluck's "First Peoples of the Tongass," an authoritative account of the original people of the region. On reading it again I find my impression confirmed. His essay has a kind of interior knowledge often lacking in reports of the Native condition and background. Other writings in this book offer us necessary data; Voluck gives us the underlying substance of place and people, without which the overall picture cannot be understood. Concerning the southeast Indian tribes and the overriding issue of aboriginal rights, he offers the most detailed account of a still unresolved issue. The two ways of thinking and living are here set forth as clearly as I have seen them.

The two Tlingit tales told here by Amy Marvin and Willie

Marks in English-language simulation of the Native story mode, are for this reader less effective than they might be if told in verse by a good poet, or perhaps written in prose by a skilled storyteller like John Straley. A brief outline can hardly do them justice, but here is an excerpt from Willie Marks' "Naatsilanei":

> They thought he would slip into the sea.
>
> Maybe that's what they wanted; if he fell into
> the sea they wouldn't help him.
> But he outsmarted them.
> He ran to the top.
> To the top, I guess.
> He ran through the sea lions.
> When he had speared about four or five of them
> > he said,
> > > "Bring the boat over here!"

The story, of a man stranded on a sea rock, abandoned by his companions to the sea lions, to be rescued by some unexpected spirit beneath the sea and returned to his wife on the home shore, is compelling, but something of the mystery and poetry is lost. The blend of Native story and contemporary colloquialisms does not work well.

I turned to John Straley's "Love, Crime, and Joy Riding on a Dead-End Road," the one piece of fiction in the book, with curiosity and anticipation. Straley, a private investigator who lives in Sitka, is well known as a writer of crime fiction. His story here, perhaps not entirely fiction, concerns a car theft and a murder, and is written with a thorough knowledge of Sitka and the Tongass. In the narrator's search for his car, his observations of the people he encounters in some ways tell us more than the descriptions of official observers. His story is brief; he writes with economy and accuracy as to details of places and persons. As he remarks at one point, "This homicide never happened, but the story is substantially true." Following on so much factual data, his story is refreshing to read, the work of a good, an honest writer. And unlike much creative writing these days, Straley's words come from a life lived, from facts known and dealt with.

I had, initially, some mixed feelings about Richard Nelson's contribution to this collection, "Heart of the Hunter." It is written in the first person, present tense mode all too common in what is now called "creative non fiction," and especially prominent in nature writing. Nelson's examination of a fresh bear dropping he comes upon in his tracking of a deer he hopes to kill may serve as an example. "To find out if this scat is as fresh as it looks, I poke two fingers far down in the glutinous mélange. And sure enough, from the surface to the very core, there's not a hint of cooling." He then imagines a thermometer inserted into the scat, which would register close to the bear's body temperature and determine how near the bear might be. His act intends to be of the same character as an early hunter's identification with the creature he is set on killing, in which every detail can be of decisive importance. But Nelson's account is close to parody.

On the other hand, his careful noting of the various clues relating to the animal's passage through the forest are those of the hunter from time immemorial. It is, as I have observed many times, like reading a book, a text in which every detail has it significance, and on which one's very life may depend. At its best, Nelson's hunting tale is a reliable guide, alert as to details, accurate as to the right moves to make in a rain soaked woodland. A hunter with less experience could do worse than to follow Nelson, step by step, through the Tongass forest. His conclusion, having killed his deer, standing by a small lake and drinking a handful of water as if in salute to the dead, is a fitting end to the hunt.

Some of the weakest writing in the book occurs in the introductory essay, "Up the Inside Passage—Bridge to the Past" by Jackie Canterbury and Cheri Brooks. It is at times less an essay than a catalogue, a listing of clichés: the far North is "frigid," the Sitka Spruce are "giant," the forests are "lush," the Tongass region is composed of "rivulets and downpours . . . from sorrowful skies," and so forth. The rest of Alaska, north of the Tongass, is "Broad, cold, inhospitable and dry." For anyone who has lived some years in interior Alaska this description is dismissive as well as inaccurate. Otherwise, their piece serves well enough as an introduction to the Tongass and contains some useful information for the uninformed.

A few random impressions: In much of the discussion here I note the inevitable abstraction that tends to afflict our writing about a place and a way of life. A good deal of the writing is at times merely informative and lacks the imaginative element that can bring a place, a forest alive in the truest sense. We have much talk of "board feet," "clear-cut stands," and "bioregions"; of "buffer zones," "harvest levels," and, a more recent term now in use, "ecotourism." The intermittent use of acronyms is in itself disturbing. We know, more or less, what is meant by ANSCA, by ANILAC, for example, but the effect on language and understanding is more severe than we realize. One feels, and all too often, that our language is not up to the task of relating us to the world. Even the word "ecosystem," in its apparent abstraction, tends to remove us from the thing itself. The difference between this way of thought and expression and the ancient identification with land and water, creatures and people, is deeply marked. Perhaps what we truly need at times is a thoughtful silence in which simply to *be*, to watch and to listen.

The Book of the Tongass, as is customary with Milkweed Editions, is beautifully designed from cover to cover. Each of the essays is introduced with a black-and-white drawing of individual plants and birds, the animals and sea life native to the region. In considering who and what really belongs here, most of us are still on the outside looking in, describing what we see, not yet a part of what is there. In her concluding essay, "The Weave of Place and Time," Carolyn Servid honestly confronts this, and acknowledges the distance she must travel from her Western intellectual origins to the rooted sense of place once common to the Native peoples. Merely writing about it, and as necessary as it may be, will not be enough. The Tlingit elder quoted by Servid from <u>A Sitka Reader</u> is explicit: "You say this is your land. Where are your stories?" Exactly so, and it is those stories, the poems and songs, together with the figurative art, that establishes for us the oneness of our humanity, as the official figures and statistics can never do. We writers and reporters, historians and critics, as illustrated by the work in this collection, continue an essential human activity.

While working on this review I was temporarily in residence on the Olympic Peninsula in the state of Washington, with the rich fall color of the maples, the alders and aspens, so vividly in contrast with the dense green of the spruce, the firs and hemlocks. British Columbia lay to the north across the straits, and beyond that lay the rain forest of southeast Alaska. Looking back in time, I could see once more the grand and brooding state park not far from Sitka, with its totems and eagles, its paths winding through the ancient forest of the Native elders. It is a unique part of our continent, though with much of its past riches of timber and fisheries sadly diminished. But the native potential remains: in the forests, the rivers, the coastal inlets, and in the seas beyond. We are now the caretakers of this land and water, and we owe it nearly everything. Our cities and suburbs, our farmlands depend upon it, as well as our playgrounds. Our understanding of this is vital, and *The Book of the Tongass* is a moving and effective reminder.

1999

Mark of the Bear:
Legend and Lore of an American Icon
(Review)

Many of us, especially in the American West, have at one time or another been impressed by a stuffed and mounted grizzly or brown bear on display in the lobby of a bank or hotel; intimidated momentarily by the enormous size and uncanny authority of the animal standing before us in its near human aspect. And with this initial impression, perhaps a sense of outrage that this imposing creature should have been killed and stuffed to adorn a scene of temporary wonder and enjoyment by people who would never willingly have confronted a bear in its own wilderness world. The more or less casual occurrence of this kind of thing has often struck me as an offense against one of the forest gods, and I have sometimes considered how much more appropriate it might be in our present world to stuff, for example, a congressman, and for public amusement place him on display—what would be the reaction to that, one wonders? But a wax museum is as close as we are likely to get.

In the splendid Sierra Club Book *Mark of the Bear: Legend and Lore of an American Icon,** we have a striking collection of photographs and essays, all concerned with one

---

*Paul Schulbert, ed. *Mark of the Bear: Legend and Lore of an American Icon* (San Francisco: Sierra Club Books, 1996).

aspect or another of the bear as it appears in our history. The photographs, by Jeff Foott, Thomas Magelsen, and Tom and Pat Leeson, as might be expected of a Sierra Club book, are outstanding, whether it is a polar bear striding the ice floes, a sleeping grizzly, or a black bear watching from a spruce tree.

There are eleven essays, by older writers like Ernest Thompson Seton and Theodore Roosevelt, as well as by more recent writers like Rick Bass and Barry Lopez, and all of them in one way or another distinctive. In a brief review one can at best summarize a few of the essays and encourage the prospective reader to seek out the whole for himself.

Seton's "Wahb" (an Indian name, we are told, for "Whitebear") follows a grizzly through a period of its life—from an early wounding, to his killing of an Indian tracker, to his growing hatred of men and their weapons, and his reputation among them as a killer to be feared. The story is old-fashioned in its diction and outlook, but remains a tale worth returning to.

In Theodore Roosevelt's "Black and Grizzly Bears" the typical headhunter and trophy killer speaks: "After several days' hunting we were still without any head worth taking home." It is an attitude taken for granted once and still common enough in Alaska and in parts of the West—that the creature is there to be hunted and killed and his head taken home and mounted, to speak for manhood or something equally dubious. We can add to this that [Teddy Roosevelt] had never before seen a live bear, even as he comments on the bears' fishing habits and its manlike digging of the ground for food, in all of which it would seem that the bear is not so different from ourselves.

With that said, it is not often that we find a president who writes so well, as in the following passage: "The woods seemed vast and lonely, and their silence was broken now and then by the strange noises to be heard in the great forests, and which seems to mark the sad and everlasting unrest of the wilderness."

In Frank Dufresne's essay, "The Twenty-fifth Bear," we meet the killer again in a hunter's search for that one possible grizzly among all others intent on killing the first man he meets. That the bear in this case had been wounded years before by another hunter only makes the final encounter more gripping.

And there is Rick Bass with his fear, honestly admitted, on finding himself too close to a sow grizzly and her two cubs, a fear muted with gratitude when the bear finally turns away and leaves him. The Montana writer Doug Peacock also tells a compelling story of being trapped between two bears, with night coming on and nowhere to go.

Gretel Erlich, in "Neighborhood Bears," describes her venture into a bear den and what she finds there, an unusual act, and one I would not have attempted. Mark Spragg's "Adopting a Bear" is a truly moving story told by someone raised to be a hunter, with a lifetime affinity for bears, and who says, quite honestly, "I hunt nothing now." His essay can be read as an elegy to the dead, the maimed, and the missing among the once vast game populations of North America, of which he remarks, "We have, for one example, unhinged the souls of sixty million bison."

I should mention also Barry Lopez's precisely written "Tornarssuk," on meeting up with a polar bear in the Chukchi Sea while on a seal hunting expedition. All of these writers, it can be said, are on the edge of things; they have not, or seldom, entered the bear himself, become part of it, as the ancient hunter was compelled in some way to do. We later people remain outside, seeking, looking, but from another world.

Finally, among the better pieces, we have Jeremy Schmidt's "Spring Tracks," and his brief meditation on finding the remains of a winter-killed bison: "Death and springtime bones in the season of rebirth. These are not contradictions, nor are they opposites. In death there is life, and in all life lie the seeds of death. Together they are an expression of continuity."

If you like to look at bears, at photographs of bears, and read about them, this is a book for you, and beautifully done. If at times one tires of looking at the photographs (we have seen many like them before), one turns to the essays and learns yet something new. The essays are blessedly free of a persistent fault in much current nature writing: an excessive attention to the narrator and to details of his or her personal life. Such writing nowadays seems all too often the outcome of looking at nature through the window of an English department office. It is refreshing to find the essays in this book focused on the outside world—on that which *is* Nature, and on one of its upstanding citizens.

With all the pictures and stories absorbed and laid aside, it seems unlikely that our fascination with bears, with so resolute totemic figure, can be exhausted. I have faced my bear more than once, have met him in the trail, had him stand before me, only to turn and run, crashing through the creek bottom or into the woods. And afterward the strange and haunted silence of something known to be there of a summer evening: a face, a track, a broken window, a deep claw scratch in the outside wall of a shed.

And once, some years ago, I had a dream in which I found myself in a log cabin with a small group of people. I was dancing with a bear, who was smiling, and we were very happy.

1997

The Fate of a River

We should be extremely alert to inflated energy predictions that have behind them the all too pervasive authority of words like "crisis" and "shortage." The crisis air that we breathe these days can be used to justify and promote all kinds of measures we may have good cause to regret later.

The characteristic slant displayed in discussions of energy policies and related matters is the all too familiar one of "use," of an exclusively pragmatic view of natural resources, and perhaps the word "resource" is itself an indication of the way we have been taught to see the world. The effect of this habitual attitude and its vocabulary is numbing and confusing; its hidden purpose, I think, is to put us to sleep, to silence in us the intelligent questioner.

No one can reasonably deny that resource management is and will be important. But beyond that I think the real concern for us will be the degree to which we allow ourselves to be manipulated into accepting programs for development and allocation—all kinds of emergency measures in fact—in the name of whatever need, actual or invented. We may end by finding that in Alaska, as well as elsewhere, the basic means for life have been taken from us by others, whether those others are embodied in government agencies or in private corporations, and we must do their bidding. And sadly enough, because of ignorance, lack of will and alertness, or simply through inertia and a conditional promise of reward, we will have handed over to those others every right of our own.

The mere creation of such a vast agency as the Alaska Power Authority is itself a threat to any local public control of resources. It seems that many people in Alaska are willing to exchange a despised federal bureaucratic control for something on the state level that may turn out to be every bit as oppressive, if not more so.

We must use things on this earth in order to live. But to see the world around us in terms of its utility alone involves us in a kind of spiritual surrender to one authority or another.

It seems likely that events in the next few years will decide for some time to come the kind of world we will have and the sort of people we will be. Recent signs of a reversal in the conservation of resources is not reassuring, but time, necessity, and common sense are on the side of conservation.

This time need not be one of continual, aggravated crises. It is possible for us to change our habits and adjust our attitudes to a new and well-founded sense of the limitations of growth and production. And if we are going to continue to speak of *growth*, then I think we need to speak of it in terms very different from those we've been used to.

A river is not killed by use, not even by a single dam. When it becomes, as many of our Western rivers have, a series of storage lakes, its character is changed, if not forever, at least through foreseeable time. Oil and sewage cannot kill a river, for these will be flushed in time. Nor is a river destroyed by settlement; humanly cared for, the houses, bridges, and fields become part of its landscape. A river dies in other and subtler ways: when it finally passes out of our consciousness as a living thing—as a force to be struggled with, or as a god to be placated and whose bounty we can harvest. It dies, as everything else must die, when we allow it to recede into that final place of dead objects: into indifference.

A river is more than water flowing.

When we come down to it, we are all native people, and the river is common to everyone, too deeply human to be erased. The fate of a river is our own fate. The flow of a river is the flow of life in us all.

1981

A Visit with a Russian Poet

It was early in November in 1966. The fall weather had so far been fairly mild, and the snowfall had been light. My first book of poems, *Winter News*, had been published earlier in the year, and had received a number of favorable reviews in various journals, and a very welcome attention at the Academy of American Poets in New York. Funds from my Guggenheim Fellowship, awarded the previous year, had made the homestead life a good deal easier, and Jo and I were more relaxed in our daily routine, with a decent supply of store bought groceries as well as from the home garden and greenhouse. We were more in touch with the outside world, but still without a phone and electric power. Mail arrived from Fairbanks daily, and we had a small battery-powered radio that allowed us to get something of the national and statewide news.

One afternoon, with the sun setting behind the Alaska Range to the south, and the light beginning to fade, I looked down from the front of the house toward the river and the highway below the homestead, and I saw something unusual: a car parked in a small clearing at the foot of the trail I had cleared some years ago to enable us to reach the highway and the mailbox that was posted some distance up the road toward Fairbanks. And very soon I saw a small group of people beginning to climb the path uphill toward the house. I was surprised, and I said to Jo: 'It looks as if we have some visitors.' And soon enough the group had reached the top of the ground near the house, and had begun to walk around toward the front door.

I went to the door to let them in, or inquire who they might be looking for. When I opened the door, an older man standing in front of the rest of the group, introduced himself: "Hello, I'm Professor (blank) from Queen's College in New York, and I've brought a Russian poet to meet you!"

My immediate thought was that someone was playing a joke, and I stood at the door, wondering what was going on. And then, immediately behind the professor, I saw this younger man who face I recognized from a photograph in a recent issue of one of the newspapers or magazines we had received. He was, in fact, the Russian poet Yevgeny Yevtushenko, who was currently on a reading tour in the United States.

I then invited the entire group into our one-room cabin. With the poet and his academic guide who was also his translator, since Yevtushenko did not speak English, were a reporter and photographer from *Life* magazine, and another reporter/photographer from *Look* magazine, two weekly publications that were very prominent at the time. We all very quickly filled the small space in the cabin, and with some shifting of chairs, clearing the sofa that was also our bed, I made it possible for us all to sit and become acquainted with one another. Yevtushenko had brought with him from the car a bottle of vodka and a smaller bottle of lime juice. I brought out glasses, and we were all soon sipping what I supposed was the customary Russian drink.

I soon understood from the scholar/translator that they were on a tour of Alaska, and that Fairbanks was but one of their visits. They had been told of me by the Academy in New York, of my writing and my remote location on the highway south of Fairbanks, and had been encouraged to make the visit. No one in the group, not even the professor from Queens, knew of my work or had seen my one published book of poems; but after having spent some brief time in Fairbanks, they decided to take part of a day and try to locate this poet who apparently chose to live in the isolation of an Interior Alaska wilderness.

So, there we were, a small group in that confined cabin space, with the woodstove heated, warming the kettle, the lamps lighted as the evening grew slowly dimmer. I'm sure I was asked many questions about our life there, how I came to choose that particular place and the subsistence living that was required in order to stay there. I had been reading at this time many Russian poets and writers, most notably, perhaps, Boris Pasternak, whose novel *Doctor Zhivago*, had been very prominent in the literary news. I had also read some of Yevtushenko's work featured in one journal or another, and I'm sure that some of this was included in our conversations.

As the time went on, I took a moment to go down into the small cellar below the cabin and bring up a bottle of the blueberry wine I had made earlier in the year. I opened the bottle and gave everyone a glass of the wine. It was cold and good, having aged many months, and all among the visiting group seemed to enjoy it, and said so with a nod of affirmation.

At some point during our conversations, Yevtushenko was asked to recite some of his verse, which he did in Russian, with what I understood to be typical physical gestures, his hand reaching toward the audience. And I was asked to read from *Winter News*. I did so in a quiet voice, choosing a couple of the opening poems from the book. I learned later that the Russian poet had remarked to his translator that "it sounded a little like prose!"

And then the afternoon turned into early evening, and the light began to fade over the river below the homestead bluffs and over the high range to the south. It was time for the Yevtushenko party to leave and return to Fairbanks. We all stepped outdoors, me with a lamp or a flashlight, and with a cheerful goodnight to everyone. I guided the party downhill to the small lot where their rented car was parked. It had been a good gathering, and I thanked them all for coming to visit.

Following on so major a break in the solitude of our homestead life, Jo and I had something new to talk about, wondering if anything else might come of that visit. A day or two later a prominent article appeared in the Fairbanks newspaper, detailing the Russian poet's visits to parts of Alaska, with numerous photographs of the poet in one place or another. There was, however, no mention of his visit to the Haines homestead, sixty-eight miles south on the Richardson Highway.

Sometime after Yevtushenko's visit there was an interesting incident in regard to the university in Fairbanks and an apparent attitude among some individuals in the English Department. There was at that time a small group of poets who were teaching there, and who considered themselves the main literary focus in Alaska, or at least the Interior Alaska region. They called themselves the "Flying Poets," who spent some part of their time flying to some of the remote villages where they gave readings of their work and in one way or another sought to promote their self-image. They had not been informed of Yevtushenko's visit, but when he arrived in Fairbanks the word got around that he was there, with a group of journalists, staying at a motel somewhere in the city, perhaps not far from the university campus.

According to information I received later, the Russian poet had told the people in New York who had arranged his Alaska visit that he did not want anything to do with a university, but simply wanted to see as much of the state as might be possible during a limited time. He and his party did their best to stay out of public and media attention, though this was not entirely possible. One of the university poets found out where the group was staying, and he went there to more or less camp on the doorstep until he could persuade the famous Russian poet to come and speak to one of his writing classes. And apparently he prevailed, and Yevtushenko did come to the university campus to spend some brief time talking to some of the students with the aid of his translator, and also give a brief reading from his poetry. A photograph of the poet with a group of university students appeared in the local newspaper with an article describing his Alaska visit. Again, there was no mention of his visit to the Haines homestead, though it is unlikely that someone in the poet's party did not refer to this during their discussions.

Remote as I was from the university environment in Fairbanks and in Alaska generally, the group of poets on campus did not know of me or my work. But when my book, *Winter News*, was published and claimed a good deal of attention in New York and elsewhere in the Lower 48, the news did reach the Fairbanks English Department and produced some major confusion among the writers there.

Who was this poet they had not heard of, living some seventy miles south of Fairbanks in a small cabin, and whose work had suddenly gained this major attention? They, as they assumed, were the center of things in the literary world of Alaska; how were they to deal with this sudden intrusion from their academic seat on the hill within the Fairbanks campus?

Well, I knew nothing of this at the time. I had never visited the university campus, had no acquaintance with anyone there, and I had little interest in the academic world of literary politics and personalities. But with my single new book of mainly Alaska poems now on the market, they finally decided to do something. Winter came on, and in early January of the following year I received an invitation to come to campus and read some of my work for their students. I no longer recall the names of the "Flying Poets," nor who it was who sent me the invitation. But I did go to read one evening in January, my first experience as a poet in a university classroom, standing before a roomful of students and dong my best (my first in many years) to present my poems and something of the background that had nourished them over the years.

Things went well, and I became acquainted with this group of university poets and writers. Later, it was proposed by the chair of the English Department that I be invited to teach something of a workshop or seminar in writing, and for a decent wage. The resident poets, however, opposed this, and the invitation was voted down. The English chair, who became a friend of ours and a frequent visitor to the homestead, was very much offended by this apparent opposition to his proposal, and he later, I understood, worked to have this small group of poets fired from the faculty.

So, a little justice, perhaps, and my work as a poet gained the attention it deserved, and not only in Alaska.

2007

Forgotten Virtues

Billy Melvin. What to say of him now after so many years? Born in rural Kansas in the early 1870s, schooled to the seventh grade, he learned to read and enjoy books, and once confided to me that he preferred Robert Burns to Shakespeare. He worked as a cattle hand in his youth, then joined the Yukon Gold Rush in 1898. Soon after, he arrived at the early settlement of Fairbanks in the Territory of Alaska, and later moved to the new mining camp at Richardson, three or four days' travel south by stage on the Valdez Trail. He built the first cabin at the mouth of Banner Creek in 1905, and remained in the Richardson-Tenderfoot area until his very last years. He was in his mid-seventies when I first knew him in the late 1940s, still active, living alone in the abandoned Richardson Post Office close to the Tanana River bluffs.

Of medium height, with a strongly hooked nose and a direct, sometimes severe look, he had the native authority of someone who had seen and endured much. He had gained no wealth, but managed to keep his honesty and survive in a difficult time. He learned to drive at age seventy, and owned an old Model A pickup truck that he drove back and forth between Richardson and his claim on Democrat Creek at the head of the Banner Creek watershed, but seldom drove to Fairbanks. For years he refused a

Social Security allowance; he did not want government money. Finally, as the years got on, he accepted a monthly check but not without some hesitation, reluctant to give up that independence of character we are unlikely to see again in our time.

For many years he and his partner, Kievic, who was originally from Russia, kept on with the mining at their claim on Democrat, long after the early rush was over and Richardson had become something of a ghost town, reduced to a handful of survivors who managed to make a living with their gold panning, their hunting and trapping. As one of the last of the original settlers, Billy was a living history of the upper Tanana region, and he had many stories to tell, to continue in some way the life he had known and of which he had been a part. Of the stories I heard him tell, the following is the one I have most vividly remembered.

One day Billy was working in the cut behind their headquarters on Democrat. Kievic was older and no longer active in the mining. Alone that day, Billy was at work on a tall ladder, picking at the rock face in search of the gold ore he knew ought to be there. In his hammering at the wall above him with his pick, he somehow loosened a large piece of the rock, which broke away and fell, striking him a sharp blow on his face and knocking him from the ladder. As he picked himself up from the stone littered floor of the cut, stunned by the blow and the fall, he knew he had been badly injured. His nose was broken, pushed to one side of his bleeding face, and he could not see out of his left eye.

He got to his feet and made his way out of the cut to the bunkhouse he shared with Kievic. He entered the doorway, still dazed, holding his nose in place as he attempted to see his way. Kievic, occupied with some kitchen chore, looked up and gasped: "My God, what happened to you?" And Billy, having recovered some of his calm, told him in a mater-of-fact voice what had happened.

And now it was time to do something to repair the damage to his face and forehead. They were a long way from a doctor: two miles down Banner Creek Road to Richardson, and then seventy miles to Fairbanks. There was no phone available. But something needed to be done, and soon. While Kievic puttered around, still in shock, Billy heated some water in a pan on their woodstove. With a mirror before him, he washed his face of the blood and dirt. He pushed his nose back into place and taped it there with a strip of adhesive. He then decided to do something about the flap of skin that still hung down over his eye, blocking his sight.

He found a sharp, three-cornered needle and some strong thread. He sat down at their kitchen table and asked Kievic to hold the mirror for him while he proceeded to sew up the wound. As he began to sew, pushing the needle through his skin while holding the loose flap in place, he noticed that the mirror had become unsteady, and he asked Kievic to please hold it still. He then looked up and saw that his partner was about to faint.

Quietly, and with the needle and thread hanging from his brow, he took his partner across the room to one of their bunks and told him to lie down until he was finished with his sewing. Billy returned to the table and chair. Having propped the mirror before him, he resumed his stitching and soon finished it. With his skin and eyebrow in place, he cut the thread, put away the needle, and, having made sure that Kievic was okay, he returned to some of the work that was waiting to be done.

Soon enough the healing took place. With his sight regained and his breathing returned to normal, Billy resumed his working life. To look at his face years later, having heard the story, you became aware of his slightly tilted nose and of the scar over his left eyebrow. It was part of who he was.

I listened to his story, one of the many he and others shared with me during that early time at Richardson, and wondered at the resolute independence of these men who took care of themselves as well as others without resort to the aid and convenience we have since grown used to. What we have gained, it seems to me, has come at the cost of an older human character that may still survive in a few isolated places on this earth, available to us once more in a time of need.

Billy Melvin died at the age of ninety-two in the Pioneer Home in Sitka, Alaska.

Fables and Distances: A Conversation
with Alaska Writer John Haines
by John A. Murray

> What's the best book about Alaska? . . . *Winter News,*
> I say, by John Haines—pure poetry; and by "pure" I
> mean poetry about ordinary things, about the great
> weather, about daily living experience.
> —Edward Abbey, "Gather at the River,"
> in *Beyond the Wall: Essays from the Outside* (1984)

Over the last two decades, one of John Haines' strongest
literary advocates has been Dana Gioia, who is currently
head of the National Endowment for the Arts. Gioia wrote
the introduction to John Haines' *New Poems: 1980-1988*
and, more recently, the preface for the critical retrospective *A
Gradual Twilight: An Appreciation of John Haines.* In the latter,
Gioia observed,

> In a literary age characterized by middle-class professionalism
> and institutional security, especially among academic writers,
> Haines reminds one of the deep, historical connections between
> the artistic vocation and voluntary poverty. . . . By spiritual
> necessity the prophetic writer must stand apart from his or her
> milieu and renounce the compromises that solicit its rewards.
> Renunciation, sacrifice and dedication . . . [permit] the sort of

freedom, candor and purity that characterize Haines' work. In a literary era dominated by institutional life, he stands out as both a singular and exemplary figure.

Haines in this context, is a distinct presence in the modern age of poetry. He moved to the territory of Alaska in 1947, homesteaded a 160-acre plot south of Fairbanks, and then proceeded to publish two dozen works of poetry and nonfiction prose, receive two Guggenheim Fellowships, and accumulate numerous other academic and creative awards. His works of poetry include *Winter News* and *The Owl in the Mask of the Dreamer*. His prose works include the essay collection *The Stars, the Snow, the Fire* and the compendium *Fables and Distances*. The entire career of John Haines, who is now in his eightieth year, may be viewed as an extended conversation with the northern landscape, as inspired by the uses of solitude, longing, and recollection.

How will the lifework of John Haines be regarded by scholars and lovers of fine literature a century from now? Haines will likely be acknowledged as the first writer of stature to emerge from Alaska. He will probably be placed among the modern American poets of nature, including Robinson Jeffers, William Carlos Williams, Theodore Roethke, Gary Snyder, and W. S. Merwin. Haines may also be seen as an independent truth teller in the tradition of Whitman and Thoreau. Above all, he will be honored as a craftsman of great personal integrity who never wavered in his fealty to place and fidelity to excellence. Gioia expressed the appeal of the venerated Alaskan icon in the following way: "Living too long in the flatlands of contemporary literary culture, we often forget that the mountains exist. They seem so impossibly distant and formidable. But despite our neglect, they remain and allow a writer brave and hardy enough remarkable perspectives. Whether or not his own age acknowledges the fact, Haines is such a writer."

The Bloomsbury Review: Could you tell us a little about your beginnings: where you grew up, your family, and when you began writing?

John Haines: As the son of a career navy officer, I was moved from place to place as my father was positioned on shore duty or at sea, mainly in the Pacific. We lived in California, Hawaii, the state of Washington, New England, and Washington, D.C. I have written of these years in one essay or another. My father was a reader, and he read to me at an early age from Rudyard Kipling, Longfellow, Thoreau, and many other writers I no longer remember. But he instilled in me a deep regard for words, for language, and for poetry as well as for stories in prose. It did not occur tome at the time that I might write, become a writer. I had, on the other hand, an early instinct for making things: for wood carving, making model airplanes and model sailing ships. In this also my father was a help, showing me how to use the tools and so forth. But it was not until my junior year in high school that I felt an early and serious interest in poetry. We were given to read Chaucer in Middle English, and I fell in love with that verse, the language, its cadence and rhyming.

During the war, while at sea in the south central Pacific, I wrote an occasional verse to amuse myself and some of my shipmates. I did not have at this time any idea that I might one day devote my life to this strange craft and art. My instincts following discharge from the navy were to begin my art studies in Washington. It was not until my first winter at my homestead in Alaska that I began seriously to write.

TBR: When not teaching, what is your life like on a daily basis?

JH: Depending on where I am and in what immediate circumstances, and aside from the daily household chores, I will be reading, perhaps making notes for something I plan to write, and writing: working at my typewriter, revising an essay or a poem, working on another draft of something in progress.

I do spend a lot of time corresponding with friends and other writers; I'm a letter writer, for sure. If I am teaching, I will spend some time with students out of class, simply visiting and trading observations on various topics, current politics, and the art itself. During the homestead years, so much of my time and energy was given to the outdoor work, it was difficult to find time for the reading and writing I wanted to do. But the life then enriched the writing in ways I was not always aware of but remain deeply grateful for.

TBR: Which do you prefer to write, prose or poetry?

JH: I have no preference at this time. For many years I thought that poetry was the one means of writing available to me, and it did not occur to me that I might write prose: criticism, book reviews, and so forth. I was afraid that if I began writing prose, I might not be able to return to poetry, to verse. This of course proved to be untrue, but it required a good deal of thought and practice for me to resolve the conflict. At times in fact the prose, though written in sentences and paragraphs, becomes a form of poetry, and I would cite parts of my essay "Days in the Field" as an example of this.

TBR: Whom have you been reading recently?

JH: I have been reading the Austrian writer Joseph Roth, his novel *The Radetzky March*, a major work. And also his journalist work in the years before World War II, and his collected stories. I've also recently read a book of the last days of the Russian poet Marina Tsvetaeva and the ordeal she went through on returning to Stalinist Russia after some years in Paris, and which led to her suicide in 1941. But I also read much journalist work in one or another paper or magazine: the *Times Literary Supplement,* the *Guardian Weekly,* and too much of our local daily newspapers, alas. My focus at the moment is on the German socialist figure Rosa Luxemburg, whose life and work I deeply admire. I wish we had her with us at this time; we need her or someone like her.

TBR: What advice would you have for someone just starting out as a writer?

JH: My advice—aside from the choices one must make as to earning a living, working at whatever most attracts one or is in some way imposed on one—is to read, as William Carlos Williams wrote to me many years ago: "Read, read, read . . . all the writers whose work you admire, and some you do not admire." But beyond that, participation in the world of people and work, and I mean that basic work we all must do in order to live, and which our modern facilities appear to make so much easier than it once was. There are no rules in this, but I think of the life of a family doctor like Williams, the varied experience of Eliot as teacher, editor, or bank clerk and the lives of so many writers elsewhere, poets who chose work in government, law, and diplomacy. And of course there is always the teaching that one may choose to do. But as I say, there are no rules in this; one must move by instinct and hope for the best.

TBR: What is your view of creative writing programs.

JH: I have recently read two very good and insightful articles on this issue: one by Neal Bowers, "A Hope for Poetry," in the Summer 2003 issue of *Sewanee Review,* and the other by David Alpaugh in an issue of *Poets & Writers* last year. Both of these take up the problem of the professionalization of poetry, the all-too-dominant presence of the M.F.A. system, the values the programs instill in so many candidates, the job market, which has rightly been labeled "po-biz." It is for me a very mixed business. I have enjoyed the time I have spent teaching in a number of programs over the years, and have been rewarded in doing so with many good friends among former students, and, needless to say, a decent if intermittent salary. But there are far too many writing programs now, and their influence has become in many respects a negative one, as an adjunct of the corporate system. We have lost that independent spirit so characteristic of poets in the past, as uncertain as their livelihoods may have been. Too many programs, too many graduates and emerging poets who tend to form a sort of clique. But others have written on this, Dana Gioia especially, with considerable insight. I remain something of a survivor from the older tradition of independence, often at risk as to a means of living, but free to write and to speak without fear of academic reprisal or loss of tenure.

TBR: What is your assessment of the current state of the publishing world?

JH: Closely related to this, and all too apparent at this time, is the reluctance of poets to speak out in that public voice once considered essential in a poet. It is difficult to imagine a Yeats or a Pope or a Dryden remaining silent on our current political situation, the war in Iraq and so much else. Our poets are confined to writing of their personal life, or of nothing at all in a verse that lacks that essential voice once common in our poets. Academic practice, with its search for tenure, has pretty well silenced that older voice. This is a loss, not only to poetry but to our common life generally. There are of course exceptions to this and, most prominently, Wendell Berry on occasion. A recent poem of his, "Look Out," has made a deep impression on me, something we badly need at this time. But all of this is a complicated issue, not merely a literary one, and not easily resolved.

TBR: Could you tell us a little about your major influences as a poet?

JH: There are many, and not necessarily literary influences, though these also are many. My years of art study early in my life had their influence and have remained so. Many of my later poems have in one way or another returned to the art to which I was attracted when still young and very involved with painting and sculpture. And there is the life I have lived, most importantly the years given to the homestead life during the 1950s and 1960s. Those years were formative in many ways. They taught me to focus on the task at hand, in which the physical translated to the pen and paper, to thought, and to words—the physical act of composing the lines of a poem. And there were, still are of course, the poets I read and continue to read, their example and success; and they are too many to list. But certainly there were Eliot, Williams, Pound, Stevens; an early influence, Dylan Thomas; and the example of many writers of prose, the novelists like Hermann Broch, Thomas Mann, Jean Giono, Robert Musil; the Scottish poet and critic Edwin Muir.

TBR: What do you think about the conventional formulation of "the burden of the past?" How does the literary past affect you as a living writer?

JH: I do not see the past as a burden—far from it. The literary past is in many respects part of an inheritance from which we must draw our examples, our potentials. I cannot imagine my own life as a writer and poet without the work I have read and learned from, continue to learn from. The past, its success and example, may appear to be a barrier only to those who lack the strength to absorb the lessons in that older work and go on to forge something new that will deepen and enlarge the tradition we must all in one way or another come to terms with and be a part of if we are lucky. It was, initially, the example of poets like Eliot, Pound, and Williams that spurred me to write in a certain way. And then came the example of classical Chinese, in translation of course, that furthered my view of the craft. My early reading in the Spanish moderns and in German poetry also enlarged my sense of what I might achieve in my own writing. The creative work aside, there are also the many texts in history and philosophy, geology, mythology, and science, the reading of which enlarges one's sense of context and the place of humanity in that larger earth history of which we are part.

TBR: Do you have an affinity for other writers from the northern latitudes, from Scandinavia, Russia, Canada, and elsewhere? If so, who in particular?

JH: For many years I felt an affinity with Nordic writers, read them and to some extent, perhaps, learned from them. The Norwegian writer Tarjei Vesaas made a major impression on me when I first read him in the late 1970s, and there are, have been, many others. My reading in recent years has ranged elsewhere, but I may for one reason or another return to some of that writing. I must say, however, that I no longer think of myself as a "northern" writer and I believe my poems in recent years have become more solidly rooted in a tradition that is broadly American and European in the widest, most basic sense.

TBR: Do you see poetry as a form of prayer, as an artifact that is something more than secular?

JH: I think my answer to this would be yes, I do at times, often in fact, feel the poem, the potential of it, to be in some way allied to, connected to, that spiritual quality we associate with prayer, and I'm certain that my early education as a Catholic had considerable influence on this. When as a boy attending Sunday Mass I listened to the priest delivering the sermon, I sensed in myself some latent power that might one day find expression in the "word": that word given to an imagined audience or congregation and which must stand for what we know as truth. I don't mean to say or imply that when I begin work on a poem or an essay that I am aware of preaching to the multitude, but I do believe that for the true poet and writer there is that potential and underlying motivation. I'm certain that Robinson Jeffers, for example, with his background as the son of a minister, had something of that motivation. His poems are, often enough, sermons for the people whether or not they are prepared to listen, and as Jeffers understood, often enough they do not listen! Yet some do, and they are the readers to whom one will speak and who are waiting, prepared to listen.

TBR: How did your early life as a painter influence you as a writer?

JH: Those years of art study deepened my sense of art in general, and its place in human history, its deep relation to religion, the apparent necessity of it, whether the art is major or merely mediocre. Most importantly, perhaps, it helped sharpen my visual sense of things, of nature: landscapes and the human presence in them. I have had since very young a keen visual sense. I loved as a child simply looking at things, whether leaves on a tree, light on the water, open fields, dark woods, or shadows. To focus on these as a painter or simply a pen-and-ink illustrator was for me inevitable. And there was also my sense of form, the object itself, which I felt necessary to grasp in some way, to make visible to others. I was attracted to sculpture in part due to the presence or potential of an object I could put my hands on to, grasp, and feel. Had I remained with the visual arts, I suspect I would have continued to work in both painting and sculpture, as many artists have done.

During the war I sketched in watercolors and with pen and ink some of what I was witness to in the warships, the many atolls and distant landscapes to be seen there in the Pacific. But I also drew on my memory of landscapes back home, imagining woodlands, birds, and animals—nature, to which I was drawn when young.

TBR: If you could have a conversation with one poet who is no longer living, who would that be and why?

JH: This is an interesting question, one I had not thought of before. There is no "one" poet with whom I can imagine speaking, exchanging views on poetry and related issues. Perhaps because he once had the grace to respond to a letter I wrote him, to meet and talk with William Carlos Williams would be something of a gift, though it might be that he would no longer like what I've written as a poet. I would like to have met and spoken with the Spanish poet Antonio Machado, whose work meant a lot to me back in the 1960s, and whose onetime village, Soria, I made a pilgrimage to when I was in Spain in 1977. I could speak to him now of what happened in Spain toward the end of his life, perhaps also of the death of his young wife in Soria, and his later flight from Spain. Among contemporaries, I would like to talk again with the poet William Stafford, a very dear friend and original writer. We had much in common in our thinking about poetry and so many social issues. A rare man and a good friend.

TBR: What do you look for in a poem that you create? What gives it life and renders it worthy of publication?

JH: This is a complicated matter, though at certain moments it might seem simple enough. There is the language, the form in which one casts it; there is the thought, the intellectual content; and there is the music, the cadence in the speech. There is often an idea, a subject, suggested by something current in the news, let's say, but also brought to attention in my reading, whether in poetry, in fiction, or in nonfiction: the thought and attention of another writer, and the example he or she might set for me. As I've had occasion to note in one essay or another, the thought and direction of a poem may require for me a considerable length of time, sometimes years, as in my "Poem Without Meaning." Despite the title, the poem does, of course, have meaning, though it required of me a long space of time to realize and define. What really matters in the end is that often elusive thing we call "truth": that the poem, the work, testifies to something we have felt to be essential in art and thought.

TBR: Do you think the Far North has replaced the Far West as the new frontier?

JH: I have come to dislike the word "frontier" as it is commonly used. It now seems to me to be outdated, though I was alive to it when younger and when I made my decision to come to Alaska after World War II. It is true, I think, that

Alaska in certain respects has replaced the West as the American frontier with all the misunderstandings and abuses that phrase contains. But I think we have outlived most of this in terms of exploration and settlement, exploitation of resources, dislocation of Native people, and so forth, though in certain respects we have not outgrown it, as badly as we need to. The true frontier now exists on another plane, another dimension. We need to learn to accept certain inevitable limits. That is, we cannot grow, expand, or develop indefinitely. We must learn to live within the limits of land and resources, to make of this a true settlement. Wendell Berry has written of this, as well as many others. It now stands at odds with our present industrial dominance, with its mania for expansion and development. But here are increasing signs that some of us, perhaps a growing number of citizens, are coming to terms with this. I do not think there will be any viable future for humankind if we cannot learn to accept certain definable limits.

TBR: What do you think initially drew you to Alaska?

JH: It was, I think, primarily the government's offer of free land to returning war veterans that moved me to come to Alaska. It was in the news at the time and impossible to ignore. I'm not certain what I might have done had not this opportunity been made available. I had always been attracted to the Pacific Northwest, having spent some time on the Olympic Peninsula as a boy in company with my father who also loved those woods and trout streams. But it was the right thing for me to do; I know that, and knew it at the time, an opportunity not likely to occur again. I have more recently thought that were I to start over again at a younger age, I might emigrate to Scotland or elsewhere in the British Isles, find a small acreage, build a cottage, and settle there, make of it a life in the old pastoral sense of this.

TBR: What do you have to say about what's happened to Alaska in your lifetime?

JH: What is missing now is that older sense of the frontier as it existed in an earlier America and which strongly characterized Alaska when I first knew it. We can no longer pretend that the frontier still exists here, no matter how often the word itself is used or misused. We have to face the fact of a changed character in the North American landscape, and learn to live with that and make the most of it. Or, perhaps we can say in a valid sense that the true frontier lies now in a coming to terms with the limits of land and resources and how we are to deal with this in the decades to come. Others, Wendell Berry most prominently, have written of this with clarity, insight, and conviction. We need now to listen and change our attitudes and our social and political behavior. Here in Alaska, as well as elsewhere, is a major opportunity to correct our past attitudes and behavior. Unfortunately, most of our "leaders" seem unable to grasp this and offer to the general public an example of understanding and renewed policy. We need something better, and we need it now.

TBR: Do you have any unfulfilled ambitions?

JH: The only ambition I now have, if it can be called that, is to finish the work I still have to do, both in prose and verse, that remains unfinished, and perhaps to clarify for myself and my readers what my hopes for poetry are in the years to come. Whether poetry, as we now have it, is up to this is a question not to be decided by me but by those to come who can return poetry to something like its ancient authority: as a voice for humanity in that larger sense we seem to have lost.

IV

POETRY CHRONICLES

Poetry Chronicle I

Of any book of contemporary poetry I would ask at least two questions: To whom is the poet speaking? Who is the audience here, actual or imagined? And secondly, what have I learned in reading this book? Has our common existence become broadened, deepened, and am I somehow changed by this reading? I would ask this of any of the books under review here, as it must be asked sooner or later of any work, now and in time to come. My questions seem all the more justified in reference to several of the books I chose not to include in this review. For what I found often enough was more of what I find all too abundantly in poetry now: in fairly ordinary language, no subject beyond this uninspiring urban self with its minor distractions, combined with a school-bred tendency to force one's poem in order to appear to have something important to say. To point up the moral, imagine Keats or Wordsworth writing verses about the bad plumbing in his house, or how scratchy his underwear felt that morning! Did William stub his toe while walking the country roads? We don't know and we do not care. Instead, consider the inspired energy of these lines from "The Simplon Pass":

> The immeasurable height
> of woods decaying, never to be decayed,

The stationary blasts of waterfalls,
And in the narrow rent, at every turn,
Winds thwarting winds bewildered and forlorn . . .

Well, we know that Wordsworth did not view that lofty pass through the lens of a television camera. He was there, on foot, with his early-nineteenth-century passion for nature and social justice—a man in all of his youthful vigor and earthbound travail. And somehow that open, receptive disposition in circumstances that offered little comfort and convenience as we have come to understand these, seems to have been at the root of much of the poetry we cherish and call great. Why this should have been so would make for an interesting study.

From the two dozen books submitted to me for review, I have chosen, not entirely at random, a short list of seven that spoke to me in one way or another something about the condition of poetry now. The books are written in a variety of modes and voices, and I have included two books by poets writing outside America: one of them a veteran South American modernist, the other an Irish poet whose work was new to me.

Richard Tillinghast's *The Stonecutter's Hand,** comes loaded with compliments from fellow poets like Richard Wilbur, Anthony Hecht, and Louis Simpson: "a wonderfully gifted poet"; "distinctive, bold and satisfying." Editorial remarks on the inside jacket echo these comments: "Richly imagined, superbly crafted," and so forth. The problem begins when we are asked to accept this kind of thing, become so commonplace now, to the point, and unfair to an honest writer, where it is difficult to take the praises seriously.

---

*Richard Tillinghast, *The Stonecutter's Hand,* (Boston: David R. Godine, 1995).

My own reaction to the poems has been mixed. While I admire the steady skill in versification, and respect the sensibility behind the poems, yet my overall impression is summed up in that word so often used to describe a certain competence: "academic." For example, there are a number of poems that derive from the poet's travel and temporary residence in Italy, Turkey, and Ireland, while periodically reverting to some domestic scene he has for the moment left behind. These poems have often a prosaic quality, as of a scholar on tour, recording various impressions clearly enough, but with little intensity of insight into what he sees and little direct participation in the lives of those who must live in that place.

Among the poems placed in Ireland, "The Ornament" is an interesting narrative concerning a troubled older woman known some years previously, and who has since died. Here are the first lines of the second stanza:

> Fine days, her troubled hair braided and pulled back
> Under a crow's wing hat, she foraged for simples
> In the nearby fields or sat in her garden aimless
> As weather, watching the robins peck
> At breadcrumbs . . .

At a later time the poet returns for a visit:

> I called on the old soul just this Twelfth Night.
> She had died two winters back, and whatever
> History brought her to these rooms died with her.

If the portrait of the woman lacks completeness and depth, the story, as developed over a page and a half, is still affecting. The equal to Yeats in lyric skill and passion it is not, nor could it be, considering the poet's presence as a periodic visitor to place and people.

From "Xiphias," a poem about, in part, an early ill-fated love affair, I quote the fifth stanza:

> I wouldn't have cared if I had driven the Fiat
> Off the cliff, so long as we went over together.
> You were twenty-two then,
> Signorina, in the south of Italy,
> And I wished I had packed a gun.

At first I thought the poem ended with this stanza, and I was considering the impact of that last line, its sudden note of finality. Then, on turning the page, I found that the poem went on for another four stanzas, and for me the final effect was diminished. I found this muted intensity to be fairly common throughout the book.

The poems shift about a good deal geographically, from Manhattan to Belgrade, to Galway, Dublin, and elsewhere. Here and there are lines, as in a brief poem called "Twos" that are merely decorative, if not plain silly:

> I leaf into a lane, thirsting for cloudburst.
> You're wet, like a gardenia.
> I speak bright plumage.
> Your breeze blows in.

Otherwise, the poems are, as they are claimed to be, well crafted, professional. It must be admitted, too, that Mr. Tillinghast's poems at times give the impression of a good deal more substance than is commonly found nowadays. Among the better poems are "Slighted in Belgrade," and "Pasha's Daughter, 1914." There are also translations from two Turkish poets. What the poems lack is something that would elevate them above mere professional accomplishment; an insight that would confirm all that they speak of so ably some central and informing idea, that which finally controls the poetry and sets it in the one unavoidable direction. Few poets have it.

Charles Rafferty's *The Man on the Tower* * is an odd book, made up of short narratives in invented voices. It is a book that at first glance, and despite a fulsome endorsement by Stephen Dunn, I dismissed as another workshop study in originality. The poems are typically placed in the first person, with the poet assuming for the moment the character of various individuals. Titles to some of the poems may give an idea of the contents: "Story of the Man Who Has Nothing to Lose"; "The Man Whose Luck Is Changing"; "Story of the Escape Artist"; "The Silent Man Speaks." In the title poem, a man, apparently on a bet with others in a nearby pub, climbs a tower, and in spite of his own fear, of the police swarming below with bullhorns, he succeeds in gaining the top, and comes down again to the cheers of the pub crowd. Is it convincing? Not entirely. For one thing, we are not told what kind of tower it is or where it is placed, and the context generally seems more than a little forced, leaving the reader asking questions.

Other poems are more convincing. Among the better is "Story of a Man Walking on the Tracks." Here are the first lines:

> He is walking the tracks, content
> to arrive where he must arrive,
> led by the steadiness of iron.

Here at least I have the sense of a man firmly placed in time, someone with a history, and who is actually walking somewhere on those tracks. Another poem, "Staying in Love," begins on a rather shocking note:

---

*Charles Rafferty, *The Man on the Tower*, (Fayetteville: University of Arkansas Press, 1995).

There is a woman you love
so you set her house on fire
late one Saturday night.

Characteristically, the poems will hint of a story behind the story being told, but we are not given anything further.

As interesting as the poems are in places, and with due credit for the inventiveness displayed throughout, I don't quite believe them. Which of the many voices is Rafferty's? Do we have the right to expect of a serious poet that he or she will present to us a convincing sensibility—a certain focus that tells us that here is someone who looks on life and experience in a certain way, and we can trust that voice and that vision? Inevitably, while reading these poems I was reminded of Wallace Stevens' "The Man on the Dump," a completely realized poem originating in a sensibility brought to bear on the life of his time in such a way that every line and every poem carries the mark of that uniqueness.

Whatever doubts one may have concerning this book, Mr. Rafferty at any rate has a gift, and it will be interesting to see what he makes of it in the years to come.

When I first looked through Annie Dillard's *Mornings Like This** and read her program notes, I was ready to set the book aside as a stunt and not worth serious attention. Subsequent reading has, to an extent, modified that impression. The book is subtitled *Found Poems*. The lines, as quoted throughout, are taken from various prose texts—from an eighth grade English text, from Van Gogh's letters, a Boy Scout handbook, and so forth—and, according to Ms. Dillard, arranged in such a way as to simulate a poem originating with a single author. In her

---

*Annie Dillard, *Mornings Like This: Found Poems,* (New York: HarperCollins, 1995).

"Author's Note" she says of the poems, "Their sentences come from the books named. I lifted them. Sometimes I dropped extra words; I never added a word." She is at least honest about her sources, in contrast to a recent perpetrator who has actually lifted whole poems from a contemporary poet, changed a word to two, and published them as his own (see Neal Bowers "A Loss for Words, Plagiarism and Silence," *The American Scholar*, 1994)

A few of her adaptations are especially effective. Among the best are those taken from the diary of a Russian naturalist, Mikhail Prishvin. Here are the last two stanzas of a poem constructed by Dillard from a walk in the woods as described by Prishvin, and to which she has given the title "Dash It":

> As for myself, I can only speak of what
> Made me marvel when I saw it for the first time.
> I remember my own youth when I was in love.
> I remember a puddle rippling, the insects around.
>
> I remember our own springtime when my lady told me:
> You have taken my best. And then I remember
> How many evenings I have waited, how much
> I have been through for this one evening on earth.

These lines are indeed poetic and moving, and might perhaps be even more so in their original context. There are others of a similar nature, such as the title poem, taken from *The Countryman's Year*, by David Grayson, and on the whole the collection has in places considerable interest. Nonetheless, what she has done here arouses some concern. What does work like this say about the legitimacy of authorship? Who in this instance is the author? Who can claim to be? I worry too about the example being set, and who might be influenced to attempt to repeat it. As it stands, it is mainly an interesting experiment;

in the hands of someone less resourceful and intelligent than Ms. Dillard, little more than a trick to be dismissed.

Walter McDonald is a poet whose work until now I have not been familiar with, but his new book, *Counting Survivors,** is of more than ordinary interest. The poems reveal, at their best, a life lived in the world of people and events, not made up in one's head to fit the occasion. The poems are about many things: his service in the air force in Vietnam, his war injuries, his children, his everyday life on the Texas plains. He calls up, memorably, a relative named Uncle Phillip, gassed in the trenches in World War I:

> I remember the tilt of his cap
> in pictures, a Texas doughboy in Paris
> caught with some girl he never saw again.

He takes his grandson hunting, and describes briefly the effect of that first kill:

> In his sleeping bag in the camper
> all night he tried to forget
> the one dove bleeding
>
> with eyes like a kitten,
> the throat rapidly beating,
> the dark pearls.

If the poems do not in all ways justify the claims made for them on the dust jacket, they are at least honest and convincing. Nowadays that can be a great deal. Here are the

---

*Walter McDonald, *Counting Survivors*, (Pittsburgh: University of Pittsburgh Press, 1995).

last lines from "War in the Persian Gulf," a poem in which he speculates on the fate of a military classmate whom he has not seen for many years:

> Where is he now,
> a general? Or sleepless in Baghdad,
> worried about grandsons, still just a captain,
> intractable, flying the slowest desk? Or shot down
> years ago in Iran, bones in forgotten sands?
> Or on alert in a French Mirage cockpit,
> his handsome face lined, lips tight,
> concealing his perfect teeth?

Allen Ginsberg, of course, needs no introduction, a popular poet if there ever was one, a name closely identified with postmodern poetry for the past four decades. His current collection, *Cosmopolitan Greetings, Poems 1986-1992,** is merely a late entry to a long list of books. I myself have always held a certain skepticism regarding this poet, even while I cheerfully affirm my respect for a poem like "A Supermarket in California." Walt Whitman has seldom appeared more contemporary.

The opening poem in this volume, titled "Preface," is a typical repetitive rant, each set of lines introduced with "I write poetry because . . ." Here are some lines from the poem:

> I write poetry because Millionaires East and West ride
> Rolls Royce limousines, poor people don't have
> enough money to fix their teeth.

> I write poetry because my genes and chromosomes fall in
> love with young men not young women.

---

*Allen Ginsberg, *Cosmopolitan Greetings, Poems 1986-1992,* (New York: HarperPerennial, 1995).

I write poetry because I have no dogmatic responsibility
one day to the next.

One is tempted to add, "I write poetry because Sylvester
Stallone is a better actor than I am," and so forth. A number of
the poems employ the same device, poems that begin with and
repeat phrases like "Research has shown . . ." or "I am Jewish
because . . .," each initial assertion followed by a catalogue
of parallels and instances. We have heard this kind of thing
before, and it is of little help now that Helen Vendler, who has
contributed for this collection a warm endorsement of the poet
and his place as a major figure, seems unable on this occasion
to distinguish the poetry from the rant, the true from the false
or half true. Whether this poet is, as she claims "responsible
for loosening the breath of American poetry at mid-century" is
debatable. From another point of view, that freeing of metric
and structure took place long before, and has been the work of
many poets, of which Ginsberg and his contemporaries, as well
as the rest of us, are the fortunate heirs.

The poems are all dated, and often the hour of their
composition is also noted. The implied spontaneity would be
enviable, were it not for the frequent impression of a poem being
either disposable or in need of drastic revision. Among the briefer
poems is one titled "Sphincter," and which begins, "I hope my
good old asshole holds out . . ." A closely related poem is about
reading a book while sitting on the toilet. Will it seem merely
churlish to complain about a poem addressed to one's anus? What
distinguishes this from any juvenile expression? Only the name,
Allen Ginsberg. Once this kind of thing might have seemed daring
in its self exposure; now it is only occasionally amusing.

If you like Allen Ginsberg, here he is, as engaging as ever
and, at times at least, as tiresome.

I have saved to the end two books I have particularly valued among those submitted to me: Joan McBreen's *A Walled Garden in Moylough,** and *Selected Poetry 1937-1990* by the Brazilian modernist Joa Cabral de Melo Neto.

McBreen is a contemporary Irish poet, and this is her second book. Until now I had not read her poems, but for me she has been a welcome surprise. Her poems are spare and precise, absolutely clear in their visual attention, her self in no way intrusive, only to the degree necessary for the voice and the point of view. Here are the final two stanzas from a short poem titled "Eanach Cuain," describing a brief past moment in a classroom:

> Impossible to know which is remembered,
> the haunted air, my mother's fingers
> tightening on my arm
>
> or the quickened beat
> of the heart when the room was still
> and filled with silence.

A slim book of fifty-two pages, forty-two poems. It has been a pleasure to read them, to appreciate that good, satisfying poems can still be written, as long as there are poets who will concentrate on the art itself and on what remains to be celebrated in the world around us. Her book deserves to be taken as a whole, but here is another poem, brief and entire, "The Clean Slice":

> Beyond the garden's solitude
> is the dark shore, hills and wind.
> A mantle covers somebody passing
> with a lantern. He turns, looks back,

---

*Joan McBreen, *A Walled Garden in Moylough*, (Brownsville, Oreg.: Story Line Press, 1995).

and in the house where he lived
sleep his wife, his children.
He drops his lantern, the light goes out,
light that once fell as warm shadows
in a summer garden on sunburned hands
and arms, on a woman's hair. In darkness
he hears their voices grow faint,
give way to silence, broken only
by the harsh sound of his son cutting
bread, the clean slice through the crust.

There it is, clean and bright, typical of the economy of McBreen's language: not a word in excess, a gift in the true sense.

As for Cabral,* my choice among these poets, my limited Spanish has been of little help with his Brazilian Portuguese. But the poems, as translated here in a bilingual edition by many hands—by Elizabeth Bishop, Galway Kinnell, W. S. Merwin, and Jane Cooper, among others—give us a fair impression of this major poet. Among the poems I admired, too long to quote here, "Encounter with a Poet" is a striking and memorable elegy in which the poet Miguel Hernandez emerges as a peasant in an arid part of Spain, his voice

not the expurgated voice
of the poet's selected works
but an edition of the wind
not found in libraries.

A voice "gone hoarse from war . . . in the dialect of dust" (translated by Richard Zenith).

---

*Joao Cabral de Melo Neto, *Selected Poetry, 1937-1990*, (Middletown, Conn.: Wesleyan University Press, 1994).

Elsewhere, a poem like "The Drafted Vulture" speaks for any minor civil servant merely doing his job, whether serving a warrant or posting an eviction notice—all part of a day's employment. Here is the second part of the poem:

> Though the vulture's a conscript, you can soon tell
> from his demeanor that he's a real professional:
> his self-conscious air, hunched and advisory,
> his umbrella completeness, the clerical smoothness
> with which he acts, even in a minor capacity –
> an unquestioning liberal professional.
>
> (translated by W. S. Merwin)

And from another poem I admire, "The Emptiness of Man," the opening lines:

> The emptiness of man is not like
> any other: not like an empty coat
> or empty sack (things which do not stand up
> when empty, such as an empty man)
>
> (translated by Galway Kinnell)

The poems are subtle and wise, the work of a man who has seen much of the world and who knows humanity. Beside such work, a Dillard appears as little more than an ambitious amateur.

Is there a lesson for us in the example of a poet like Cabral? I am thinking here of his varied career as a diplomat and administrator, of his many activities outside literature, and which compares, for example, with the career of the Finnish poet Paavo Haavikko, a man of the world and his time in every sense, experienced in business and the theater, in many additional fields, and whose poems are seriously adult when compared with their typical American counterpart. I think too of the Icelandic poets whose work I have come to know: editors and journalists, librarians and engineers, only occasionally a teacher, a professor.

Participation in the world enlarges and deepens the potential poetry, the potential man or woman, and is especially needed now when so much of our common life is narrowed and restricted by a nearly universal specialization. There are, surely, no absolute rules, but the picture of thousands of graduates scribbling verses, or prose, sporting a merit badge that says *Poet*, and with hardly a clue as to their professional isolation—of the cultural forces that inevitably convert them into members of a fringe, a subculture of society—ought to give more of us a moment of pause and reflection. When confronted with the pathology of so much current poetry, its characteristic self-absorption, how refreshing, in the instance of a McBreen or a Cabral, to be able to focus on the poetry and consider its source in the world at large—on the way in which good work, rather then leaving us mired in juvenilia or mental illness, returns us to that world a little more wakened in our senses, confirmed perhaps in a certain faith in existence itself.

Poetry Chronicle II

Invited as guest speaker to the annual Robinson Jeffers Conference in Carmel earlier this year, I had occasion once more to reflect on that poet's life and thought, on his expression of that thought in a language that might speak to Everyman, as was once the custom, if not an absolute necessity, for a poet in the past—a passion now largely lost to American poetry. As I noted in my Jeffers talk, there are other modes for poetry, and the lack of a direct address of social and political issues does not necessarily condemn a given work. It is, however, a factor I believe a critic now should be aware of, that the reader also may be aware of it.

Among the more interesting books I received for review is Davis McCombs' *Ultima Thule,** chosen by W. S. Merwin for the Yale Series of Younger Poets. A dictionary definition of "Ultima Thule" defines it as "any faraway, mysterious place . . ."; or, in McCombs' words, "a mapless place." The poems are concerned primarily with Mammoth Cave in Kentucky, its geology and human history, and as told in part in the assumed voice of a slave, Stephen Bishop, who served as a guide to the

---

*Davis McCombs, *Ultima Thule,* (New Haven, Conn.: Yale University Press, 2000).

cave in the mid-1880s, and whose explorations of the cave resulted in a number of important discoveries.

My initial impression of the book was of a creative writing project, perhaps a graduate thesis, in this case making use of the life and work of a dead person in order to advance one's career. It is done often enough these days, and who's to object? Here are the opening lines from one of the poems:

> A hot night, and the first breeze through my window
> carried with it the whinny of a horse.
> It had been so still, but suddenly then night
> was restless, cocking its ear to a distant
> crackling,
> a light, as of dawn, across the valley.
>
> ("Brush Fire")

Am I to believe that these are the words and thoughts of a Kentucky slave in the process of learning to write? Or are they the words of a young writer who has chosen a theme to exploit? These are not idle questions.

The poems in the opening section are satisfactorily written in the chosen sonnet form, unrhymed, the meter at times irregular. A shift, in section II, from the sonnet to an extended free verse, hardly changes the tone of voice, no longer that of Bishop:

> What an ancient sea set down in even lines
> is worked into a cursive scrawl,
> as run-off through the bedding planes
> recalls
> a steamy day, an inland sea,
> the continent adrift—
>
> ("Flowstone")

Which reads, in spite of the cadence, rather like a

guidebook prose excerpt. In the third section of the book the form shifts back to the sonnet and to a voice that appears to be McCombs': "Some nights I drive the back roads out across/the country, its knobs and barrens spreading . . ."

Taken poem by poem and line by line, the writing is clear and to all appearances accurate as to details of the cave and the people involved in its history. It is useful to know, by the way, that McCombs has worked as a park ranger in the Mammoth Cave area and presumably knows it well. What is missing, for this reader, is a necessary passion of poetry, a dramatic element that would bring the narrative to life in some way now lacking. In speaking of the means of lighting then used in the caves, a device referred to as "the Bengal Light," McCombs, in Bishop's voice, writes as follows:

> How sad I grew
> to see the changes wrought in them by sunlight.
> How lusterless they appeared under glass,
> their sparks extinguished, their music fled.
>
> ("Dripstone")

This is the voice of an English poet, an echo from the classics, if not in all ways convincing. Later, in a poem near the end of the book, Bishop's mysterious death at age thirty-six is quietly noted, the voice now that of McCombs:

> I went that drizzling night to stand
> where the paper trail he left had vanished:
> woodsmoke, mist, a mossed-over name.

This has not been an easy book to come to terms with. Despite the doubts expressed here, I have enjoyed reading the poems, and perhaps learned something in doing so. I believe, however, that some needed resolution in the use of the voice would make for a significant improvement. Precisely what that voice should be, what it might sound like, I can't be certain, and it would be a matter not easily resolved. *Ultima Thule*, whatever its flaws, is a first book, one that holds some serious promise.

I have enjoyed reading Robert Phillips' new book, *Spinach Days*.* I was at first skeptical of the title and the random, whimsical nature of his subjects with no discernable underlying theme. But his skill in the verse forms he has chosen seems to me exceptional, whether it is the rhymed quatrains of the title poem, or the more or less free verse of "Things" with its direct reference to W. C. Williams:

> No ideas but in things,
> said Doc Williams.
> Christ! I must have
> an awful lot of ideas
> God knows I have
> an awful lot of things.

Indeed, and he has also a lot of subjects. There is a poem to his prostate; another titled "John Dillinger's Dick," with its amusing account of the gangster's lost sex organ found preserved, according to one source, in the basement of a funeral home. There are "Found Poems," adapted from letters by Emily Dickinson, Van Gogh, and others; a moving eclogue for Amy Jones, someone whose life and person the poet remembers and records:

> for old-time's sake I drive down Sorrel Road.
> The rustic road sign should surely be changed.
> With you not there, Sorrel transliterates into Sorrow.

---

*Robert Phillips, *Spinach Days*, (Baltimore: Johns Hopkins University Press, 2000).

The poems are in most cases entertaining, if sometimes no more than that. I've been tempted to describe the whole as middle America at its most typical: the old car, the family wash, the neighborhood ball park, and so forth. At times, perhaps, a search for something to write about, and a certain amount of self-conceit. The title poem, however, is excellent, a personal and family history awakened by the smell of spinach being cooked:

> The odor of cooking spinach
> brings them back: summer
> evenings, the world's richest
> city, Manhattan before my senior year . . . .

A poem on the destruction of the old Pennsylvania Station in New York is one I will remember, as I remember the grand old building itself, before, as Phillips writes, "it fell to greed." Another striking poem is also one of the shortest, and I will quote it here:

> Her mother brought her down
> to the laundry room. Picking
> the wicker clothes basket
> she explained, "You must separate
> the colored from the white."
> And they did. Their black maid,
> ironing in the corner, nodded.
> ("Early Lesson")

It is a poem in which something of our troubled social history is briefly clarified in a way that no news column can equal—one of the virtues of the art of poetry when seriously practiced.

It was refreshing for me to read that Judy Jordan, the author of

Carolina Ghost Woods,* comes from a family of sharecroppers and has herself spent time working in the fields in the Carolinas. That she has in recent years gained academic degrees in poetry and fiction does not lessen my interest in her writing. Behind that writing lies a true, earthbound experience, and at it most effective that experience comes alive in the poems:

> Geese lift from the far hill in the last light,
> unfurl above the alders, dip and scrape across the
>   pond,
> and I don't know how much longer I can wait
> as the wind, smelling of leaf rot and dung,
> tugs the evening over this darkening land.

I might question that the geese "unfurl" in their flight, but otherwise I can feel here the presence of someone who has, as we say, been there.

In preparing for this review, what I found in a number of books was simply a good deal of prosy, mediocre writing, a colloquial sameness of tone, and often enough a strained effort to appear to be original when it was obvious that the writer had next to nothing of importance to say but was pursuing a career project in creative writing. There is little in Jordan's work as consistently bad as some of the writing I encountered in a book I chose not to review here, Molly McQuade's *Barbarism*, with lines like "I'm a pilgrim frugging in the locks of resin," or "the gooey horsehair virus of what and stop . . ." a language promoted by careerist politics and which only appears to be original.

Jordan's writing is of a more serious nature, yet even there I come on expressions like "In the moon fade and the sun's puppy

---

*Judy Jordan, *Carolina Ghost Woods: Poems*, (Baton Rouge: Louisiana State University Press, 2000).

breath . . ." ("Help me to Salt, Help Me to Sorrow"); or "in the shrink of light" (from "Scattered Prayers"). In a poem on the twenty-fifth year of her mother's death we find this line: "and light sifts slow across field fetch . . ." which sounds as if it might have been written by Charles Wright. Yet Jordan has her ghosts and her story, her poems an effort at recovery of lost times and people. The title poem is a major one in this respect, with perhaps more promise than success, momentarily distracted by its opening stanza:

> A crow calls and the sunset smears into questions
> That swing with the cow's hoof, reflect in fire,
> And wait under the wing with the thin lips of death.

There is, and increasingly so, a manner of writing that calls attention to itself and into which the true subject disappears with hardly a trace. Another stanza further on in the poem is much better:

> Tonight the clock is meaningless
> and I'm still a child on the back steps,
> my father gone into the woods to kill himself
> while I wait for the single shotgun blast,
> an echo of the wood's echo . . .

At their undistracted best, as in "Hitchhiking into West Virginia," and in spite of an awkward opening line: "Even here in this dabbed and scumbled distance," I sense the actual presence of both place and person:

> Either way, it's a narrow stretch of road.
> The ground, without light to give it form,
> Rises against my feet,
> And rocks and trees brush past before words can
> Mean anything.

It is those words, however, and their meaning, that we look for and expect to find in a true poem.

Mark Jarman's *Unholy Sonnets** might be described as a hectic, driven search for a viable God, and in fact the title of the book pretty well sets the scene and pace. The opening poem, a prologue to the extended sequence and an initial address to a presumed God, reads in part as follows:

> Please be the driver bearing down behind,
> Or swerve in front and slow down to a crawl,
> Or leave a space to lure me in, then pull
> Ahead, cutting me off and blast your horn.
> ....
>
> Lurching onto the shoulder of the road,
> And get out, raging, and walk up to me,
> Giving me time to feel my stomach drop,
> And see you face to face, and say, "My Lord!"

This is very much an American God being spoken to, armed and dangerous. The writing is also close to parody, or can be read as such. Contrary to my initial impression, however, which was of a lot of talk and a random violence that went nowhere, Jarman's book has proved to be a provocative one: a search for a god who does not exist, or no longer exists. As Jarman says in the third sonnet of his sequence, "My thoughts about you are derivative." What is conveyed throughout the book is a struggle with an absence, a possible god, and a vacancy: "The grave is empty. Last night it was full."

The sonnet form is adhered to, and skillfully so, the rhyme intermittent. The essential thing being clarified here is

---

*Mark Jarman, *Unholy Sonnets: Poems*, (Ashland, Oreg.: Story Line Press, 2000).

the spiritual void that is present-day America. In one of the sonnets Jarman touches on a pervasive fact of our times: the radio voice, the newscast, the media-face—all of which pretend to speak a truth and instead bear witness to a poverty:

> The devil comes on the airways, crooning
> Soft Christian rock songs in a cartoon voice,
> Loops of self-love and pity wound through swooning
> Melodies stamped from saccharine and noise.
>
> I'll have to find a way to turn it off
> Or change the channel, let alone my life.
>
> (#19)

Collectively and at their individual best, the poems draw a forceful attention to the absence of a serious and fulfilling belief. Reading these poems, considering their occasions, one understands why T. S. Eliot, following on his journey through "The Waste Land" and other poems of his early period, turned in the later work to the Church and found consolation there. In certain respects that life and work can be seen as a parable for our time. I have also thought of Rilke while reading Jarman, selections of poems from the *Book of Hours,** as translated by Babette Deutsch:

> You, neighbor God, if sometimes in the night
> I rouse you with loud knocking, I do so
> only because I seldom hear you breathe
> and know: you are alone.

In Rilke's address to his God there is a tenderness, a

---

*Rainer Maria Rilke, *The Book of Hours,* trans. Babette Deutsch, (Norfolk: New Directions, 1941).

sweetness, lacking in Jarman, whose god is at times more like a traffic cop or a gunman: "Before he enters the quick stop and reveals / The weapon he will use to beat or kill"

Finally, to cite another brief comparison, and while I respect Jarman's efforts toward recovery of a truly religious life in our distracted and impoverished age, I find a more deeply spiritual quality in these concluding lines by the German poet Johannes Bobrowski*:

> Were there a God
> And in the flesh,
> And could he call me, I would
> Walk around, I would
> Wait a little.
> ("Always to Be Named")

These lines, and the poem from which they are taken, may speak directly to Mr. Jarman, too often inclined to force what cannot be forced.

The title poem of Stanley Plumly's *Now That My Father Lies Beside Me, New and Selected Poems, 1970-2000**,* is among the more satisfying I have read recently and can serve as an example of this poet at his best:

> We lie in that other darkness, ourselves.
> There is less than the width of my left hand
> Between us. I can barely breathe,
> But the light breathes easily,
> Wind on water across our two still bodies.

---

*Johannes Bobrowski, *Shadow Land,* trans. Ruth and Matthew Mead, (Chicago, Alan Swallow, 1966).

**Stanley Plumly, *Now That My Father Lies Down Beside Me, New and Selected Poems, 1970-2000,* (New York: Ecco Press, 2000).

The poet's father has been dead for many years, and their imagined meeting, lying together in that darkness, is all the more effective for our understanding of that fact. The poem is placed at the end of the book, to close off an unusual sequence: the poems reading, front to back, from the most recent to the earliest, and without the customary return to memories of his father and mother, to the places he lived as a boy, the house he helped his father to build, the stray dogs that sometimes frequented the neighborhood, and much else. One thing I have especially liked in Plumly's poems is his reclaiming of his family history in rural Ohio. It seems clear that this part of his early life remains at the roots of his creative work:

> If I have to choose I choose those nights
> I sat in the dark in the Mote Park
> outfield waiting with my father
> for the long fly balls that fell more
> rarely than the stars . . . .
> ("Men Working on Wings")

Other poems from this selection from six previous volumes move some distance from that Ohio homeland. "Farragut North," a poem written in what appears to be an irregular hexameter, is placed at a Metro station in Washington, D.C., where the nation's homeless are often camped and whose condition reminds him of his mother's generosity toward the people who in an earlier period came to the door of their home in search of help at a difficult time:

> To her each day was the thirties. The men at
>   the door had
> the hard boiled faces of veterans, soldiers of
>   the enemy.
> My mother saw something in them, homelessness

> the condition
> of some happiness, as if in the faces of those
> drifters could be
> Read pieces of herself still missing . . .

But now, for the poet at this later time, "their isolation is complete, like the dead or gods."

Spaced at intervals are four prose poems, each of them among the more satisfying in the book. There are also four poems concerned in one way or another with the poet John Keats, a figure for whom Plumly seems to have special affection: "He lies in the artist's paradise / in Rome, among the pagan souls . . ." ("Constable's Clouds for Keats"). I have returned to another compelling poem, "In the Old Jewish Cemetery in Prague," with its universal and lasting associations: "Stone is the shade of memory, / snowfall, dust, the piling and the drift."

Now That My Father Lies Down Beside Me is a book to be read slowly, to be returned to and thought about.

Nearly alone among the books I have read recently, the poems in D. Nurkse's *Leaving Xaia* * return me to the names and events of our time, and do so in a way quietly affecting. His poems are among the few I have read that escape the self-absorption of so much current writing. They deal with the world at large: the bombed city, the homeless child, the border, the checkpoint:

> Once
> they took your papers
> and you felt your soul dying
> but they brought them back
> with a neat stamp: war zone.
> Behind their dusty epaulettes

---

*D. Nurkse, *Leaving Xaia,* (Marshfield, Mass.: Four Way Books, 2000).

you glimpsed a city
that never quite ended.
("The Checkpoints")

To escape the persistent small self of the ego: a difficult task in our present society, and one must have a subject, something beyond the self and which, perforce, includes the self. Nurkse in these poems appears to be one of the few. It is worth noting that he has written widely on human rights, and on the evidence of these poems has also traveled widely in countries where those rights have been long under threat. That background is obvious enough in the poems and contributes to their quiet passion and conviction.

The first third of the book is taken up with the story of a failed marriage, but even there it is the everyday events and details,

the "neighborhood of butcher shops,"
"the clerk's thumb
finding an empty page
in the greasy ledger"

that bring the poems to life. An extended stay in the hospital does not alter this:

All praise to the mask
Who healed me with a knife.
Now I pray for patience
Until the light changes.
("A Block North of Mercy")

In reading Nurkse I recognize the world we live in, the conflicting times we share, whether we are entirely aware of it or wish to admit it. The voice in these poems does not call attention to itself in the use of distorted language, yet it speaks to us, here and now:

> And you realize you were home
> There, in front of the windows,
> Those were the golden cards
> Dealt you: when you walk back,
> That street—if it is the right street –
> Is dark like all the others,
> But you hear the whimpering of the child.
>
> ("Lateness")

There are no extra words in these poems. They speak quietly, with an inner authority, and to which we should listen.

By way of closure, I would like to mention a book not formally reviewed here, and recently issued by Salmon Publishing of Ireland. *Autumn in the Alaska Range,** by Tom Sexton, is a gathering from six previous collections. The poems are mostly brief, influenced in some respects by the classical Chinese of Tu Fu, and quietly impressive in the clarity of their imagery. Amid the wordy clutter of so much current verse, I have found the poems refreshing to read. Sexton has been writing, mainly about Alaska, for many years. Since retiring from teaching at the University of Alaska, Anchorage, he has until recently served as Poet Laureate of Alaska.

---

*Tom Sexton, *Autumn in the Alaska Range,* (Cliffs of Moher, County Clare, Ireland: Salmon Publishing, 2000).

Poetry Chronicle III

There is a sound, a tone, or a pulse, if we can put it that way, which in any period underlies the more obvious music of verse, and that is the sound of the larger world around us—of forces veering and connecting, the flaring of wars and passions, the untimely dissolution of societies, collision and breakage—all of which constitute the world in which we must construct our lives and shape our thought. To the extent that the language and its structures reflects these forces, it serves us with a certain truth.

In reading Wallace Stevens, especially late Stevens, one finds a mastery that is not simply a mastery of form and technique, though that is there also, but a mastery of another sort, that of one's time, of the hour in which one lives and works. I am speaking of that which animates the work of a certain period—call it geist, spirit, or something else, it is what makes the difference. One can be schooled to recognize it, but it cannot be faked or invented. It is present or it is not, and its appearance cannot be predicted.

The foregoing thoughts have been much in my mind while considering the work under review here. Henry Taylor's new collection, *Understanding Fiction,** is a case in point. The titles and

---

Henry Taylor, Understanding Fiction, (Baton Rouge: Louisiana State University Press, 1996).

141

subjects of the poems tell us a great deal: "After a Movie," "Night Search for a Lost Dog," "Elevator Music," and "Free Throw." There is a poem about a child's popped balloon; another about a horseshoe game; a brief memorial poem for the poet William Stafford; another for E. A. Robinson. "Flying Over Peoria," a poem I liked as well as anything in the book, opens with these lines:

> The man beside me nudges my arm
> and shrugs toward the window.
> "Peoria," he says. I glance across him
> at clouds and vague patches of earth.
> "Where many things won't play,"
> I say, trying to smile.

The poem continues with a brief account of an episode in the man's life, and ends with these vaguely consoling lines:

> A man weeps
> privately, another ponders
> odd uses of a word like *concept,*
> and below them the featureless landscape
> keeps slipping away.

The poem is affecting in a quiet way: a momentary encounter with another human being that might happen to any one of us in the odd, often dislocated travel of our time. The poems otherwise are ably written in a variety of metrical forms, dominated by domesticity and locality—the poems of a country gentleman, in fact. A compelling book, on the whole, it is not. And then, in a short middle section with the heading "Five Translations" I come on a poem by the Bulgarian poet Kiril Kadiiski, and from which I quote the last stanza.

> Like beads of sweated blood, stars wink and fail;

the poplar holds a vinegar moon on high.
An aerial thrusts its arms into the sky –
a cross to which the living world is nailed.

("Good Friday")

In what I take to be an accurate translation, we are for the moment in another world altogether. Though no specific place is named, in the starkness of that final image the note is unmistakable, and it is our modern world, become increasingly universal in its menace and encroaching violence. It is a note not to be found elsewhere in this book.

Among the books considered for this review I have been pleasantly impressed by David Wagoner's *Walt Whitman Bathing*.* If I did not know that Wagoner is writing from the Pacific Northwest, I would discover in his poems, and not withstanding the titles and subject matter of many of them, a tone and sensibility that is clearly not eastern nor Midwestern, but centered on the western rim of the continent, in a wet and rainy land. The poems are otherwise varied, the attention shifting from one scene to another. There is a poem about his father "Laughing in the Chicago Theater"; another about his school days; another about some trouble with his eyesight. There is humor, as well, in a poem about a meeting between Aldous Huxley and Thomas Mann on a beach in California, and what they inadvertently find there. One of my favorites, "Walking Around the Block with a Three-Year-Old," is a delightful poem about the poet's young daughter, what they find on their walk, and the interrupted conversation between them.

She sees a starling legs up in the gutter.
She finds an earthworm limp and pale in a puddle.

---

*David Wagoner, *Walt Whitman Bathing: Poems*, (Urbana: University of Illinois Press, 1996).

"What's wrong with them?" she says. I tell her they're dead.

On their way home they find that the starling has disappeared. "Where did it go? / She says . . . I show her my empty hands, and she takes one."

The title poem is also moving in a quiet way, being a description of Whitman in his late, disabled years, bathing alone in a pond near his home. Throughout the book are poems on specific places. "On the Forest Floor," in the final section of the book, is one of the more rewarding poems I have read recently, marked by an observant intelligence and a sober grace in expression. The last stanza is a follows:

> The closer you look at it, the more it changes
> To the landscape of the earth.
> The yet-to-be and the dead and the newly risen
> Merged into rootless lives whose entrances,
> Like your lost eyes, become what enters them,
> Where all that endures is your bewilderment.

One might say of such woodland poems that they are the work of someone for whom that world is a place to visit as part of a weekend venture, and return from to a safe harbor. For this reason, perhaps, Nature, as felt and witnessed here, has a sometime distant aspect. Yet the felicity with which Wagoner writes may have its permanent attraction. The poems justify themselves on their own merits, and the best of them have a genuine, true attention to the world around them; the poems of someone who has looked intensely at the shrubs, the flowers, and at the forest floor from which they have sprung.

Anthony Hecht's *Flight Among the Tombs** has received high

Anthony Hecht, Flight Among the Tombs, (New York: Alfred A. Knopf, 1996).

praise from a number of reviewers. It is in many respects an impressive work, and I have found it entertaining in the best sense of the word. The poems in the major portion of the book, composed in various voices and figures of *Death*, and illustrated with' wood engravings by Leonard Baskin, are particularly compelling. Whether the work places Hecht among the great writers of our time, as proposed in the jacket comment by Harold Bloom, is another matter and not to be decided here.

Titles to some of the poems will give an idea of the direction of the writing: "Death the Oxford Don"; "Death the Painter"; "Death the Inquisitor," and so forth. "Death the Judge," in these concluding lines

> . . . has composed
> His predetermined sentence,
>
> And in his chambers sits
> Below a funeral wreath
> And grimaces and spits
> And grins and picks his teeth.

If at times the work leaves the impression of Death on a holiday—rather like a Day at the Races, or a Night at the Opera—still, the underlying sinister tone and the many vivid personifications of Death are often arresting. It is a tribute to Mr. Hecht's mastery of formal verse that poems like these, in other hands perhaps all too occasional, succeed here in being far more than that. His traditional training and exercise stand the poet in good stead. Even when one has for the moment little of overwhelming importance to say, the presence of the craft and discipline in itself may rescue the writing from inconsequence.

This artistry is not without defect. In the second part of the book a memorial poem for James Merrill is moving in its evocation of that admired figure. Another for Joseph Brodsky, though it displays an obvious affection for the man and writer, is more problematic. Whatever else that poet may have been, he was not "American" in any deeply valid sense.

One or two of the poems in this section seem at times excessively artful or merely decorative. A few lines from "La-Bas: A Trance" may illustrate this:

> Harems of young, voluptuous, sloe-eyed
> Houris, undressed, awaiting his commands,
> Untiring courtyard fountains casting jewels
> Thriftlessly into blue-and-white-tiled pools,
> Their splashes mingled with languid sarabands.

A high-class art, if you will, not entirely free of excess.

In Donald Justice's *New and Selected Poems**we have the example of an unfailing mastery of verse. Many of the poems are by now well known and to be found in influential anthologies. An early poem, "Here in Katmandu," can serve as a more than adequate example, with its opening and concluding stanzas:

> We have climbed the mountain.
> There's nothing more to do.
> It's terrible to come down
> To the valley
> Where, amidst many flowers,
> One thinks of snow,
>
> Meanwhile it is not easy here in Katmandu,
> Especially when to the valley
> The wind that means snow
> Elsewhere, but here means flowers,

---

*Donald Justice, New and Selected Poems, (New York: Alfred A. Knopf, 1995).

Comes down,
As soon it must, from the mountain.

Among other poems from an early period, "On the Death of Friends in Childhood" continues to echo in its concluding grace and regret: "Come, memory, let us seek them there in the shadows."

Yet, and while acknowledging the very genuine accomplishment to be found here, and for which we are to be grateful, something is missing, and that something is a necessary tension between the poet and society, in this instance a situation resolved perhaps a little too comfortably. A more recent poem, "Pantoum of the Great Depression," may serve as a useful illustration. Here is a representative stanza:

We gathered on porches; the moon rose; we were poor.
And time went on, drawn by slow horses.
Somewhere beyond our windows shone the world.
The Great Depression had entered our souls like fog.

Here, in the exercise of a particular, complicated verse form, the very skill involved in its practice may tend to diminish the potential subject. In this poem there is no real poverty, but rather distance and nostalgia. And it may be that the true subject of our time will require another approach, another sort of mastery.

Finally, as seems reasonable when reviewing the better part of a lifetime effort, to what extent can one describe a growth in these poems? An early mastery, yes, but beyond that? I am not certain we find here that slow maturing of outlook that in Stevens, for example, found expression in so late a poem as his elegy for George Santayana, "To an Old Philosopher in Rome," a poem that in its gravity and resonance seems to sum up an entire epoch. But such things are rare at any time, and in considering Donald Justice we must be grateful for the outstanding work we find here.

Concerning two other books I will be brief if not merciful. C. K. Williams' *The Vigil** reveals, mainly, a good deal of inflated writing. An introductory poem, "The Neighbor," sounds a typical and repetitive note:

> Her five horrid, deformed little dogs, who incessantly
> > yap under my window;
> her cats, God knows how many, who must piss on her rugs –
> > her landing's a sickening reek . . . .

It would be easy to skim through this book and make a catalogue of the ludicrous and outrageous, the absence of a worthwhile theme, the need to force, to invent subjects and occasions in order to justify another book and further a career. The final impression is that Williams has for the most part no true subject, and must rely on the sprawl of his lines to compensate.

> Beds squalling, squealing, muffled in hush; beds pitching,
> > leaping, immobile as mountains;
> beds wide as a prairie, strait as a gate, as narrow as the
> > plank of a ship to be walked,
> *I squalled, I squealed, I swooped and pitched; I covered*
> *my eyes and fell from the plank.*
>
> > > > ("The Bed")

The italics only serve to emphasize the theatrical nature of the writing.

"In Darkness" is a more promising poem that revisits

---

*C.K. Williams, The Vigil: Poems, (New York: Farrar, Straus, & Giroux, 1998).

Harlan County, Kentucky, and the condition of its coal miners earlier in this century. Yet even here the potential in the subject is dissipated in Williams' apparent need to inflate both occasion and language: "as now, they, the political thugs, crazed with power, waiting to wreck social mayhem . . ." Were there space in this review, it would be instructive to compare the poem with Malcolm Cowley's sober account of being there at that decisive moment in the early 1930s:* the utter conviction with which Cowley and his fellow writers confronted the enormity of the social abuse, and the tepid sympathy invoked by Williams in his verses.

The one thing that at times redeems the writing is the onrush of the verse lines that would carry all before them, good and bad, trivial and genuine. I come away with the impression of a poet who simply hurls himself into the writing of a poem, come what will. I can be persuaded to admire this, up to a point; but the volume of fluff and buffoonery can be more than a little discouraging. Despite the sprawl of his lines on the page, inviting comparison, Williams is no Whitman; he has no expansive nation or suffering people to fuel his sensibilities and his verses, only his own kitchen and bedroom.

Dave Smith's *Floating on Solitude,*** a gathering from three previous volumes, announces itself with this comment from Helen Vendler: "I scarcely know where to begin in describing Smith's rich writing . . . his poems make other poems seem loose, unfinished." We are then invited to savor poems that begin with lines like these:

---

*Malcolm Cowley, "Radical Images," The Portable Malcolm Cowley, (New York: Viking, 1990).

**Dave Smith, Floating on Solitude: Three Volumes of Poetry, (Urbana: University of Illinois Press, 1996).

The sun frets, a fat wafer fallen like a trap of failed
    mesh.
    ("Hole, Where Once We in Passion Swam")

It squats in a grandmotherly yard,
surrounded by the breaking teeth
of a fence . . .
    ("Chinaberry Tree")

Your fat wife weeps through her yellow shawl.
By bricks furred with soot your ragged cat laps from
    a bottle . . .
    ("Undertaker, Please Go Slow")

With lines like these, with entire poems fashioned of
similar material, who needs vaudeville? There may be better
things in Smith's overweighted 320-page collection, but
you will look hard to find them. If you wish briefly to be
entertained by some obviously comic language, by a variety of
self-parody, or by a mock-country usage, then Smith is your
man.

Am I at home here, humpback snub,
       nub of nothing, rock where pines
preen on wimpling winds,
       roots with capillaries bulged,
sucking seamist to live? I oar out
      anyway . . .
    ("Eastern Shore, Smith Island")

And so on page after page. Then what to make of Ms.
Vendler's extravagant praise? Certainly, a failure of critical
judgment, and beyond that a sign of something weirdly amiss
in contemporary letters.

I should perhaps defer speaking of poems in a language I do not know and cannot read, but the poems of the Hebrew poet Yehuda Amichai* as translated by Chana Bloch and Stephen Mitchell, have offered a useful means of comparison with the work of a few of our more immediate American contemporaries. In returning partway to my opening remarks I must again refer briefly to the poetry of a place and a situation all too representative of our present world, and which in these poems has been written of with so much insight and passion.

> And so farewell to you, who will not slumber,
> for all was in our words, a world of sand.
> From this day forth, you turn into the dreamer
> of everything: the world within your hand.
>
> Farewell, death's bundles, suitcase packed with
>   waiting.
> Threads, feathers, holy chaos. Hair held fast.
> For look, what will not be, no hand is writing;
> and what was not the body's will not last.
>
>   ("Farewell")

Here, subtly imprinted, is the unmistakable tone and historical burden, of which one can say: This is our time, this speaks for all. "Beautiful is the world that wakes up early for evil . . ." ("In the Middle of This Century"). It is not the only world we know, but it is one of which we must somehow speak, hold in conscience—or, it may be, remain silent before it. And the silence so common among us, in spite of our books and our talk, is heavy, dense with memory and premonition.

---

*Yehuda Amichai, *The Selected Poetry of Yehuda Amichai*, trans. *Chana Bloch and Stephen Mitchell*, (New York: Harper and Row, 1986).

And silently, like a doctor or mother, the days
  bent over me
and started to whisper to one another, while the
  grass
already was laid flat by the bitter wind
on the slope of hills I will never walk again.
   ("Travels of the Last Benjamin of Tudela")

A poetry quietly eloquent with the pain, the losses, and displacements of our time, in which one writes with the only instrument at hand.

While considering the books for this review I have had in mind a recent newspaper photograph of a street in Grozny, in Chechnya, a scene of almost total ruin: buildings shattered and gaping, trolley lines torn up, streets clogged with debris, a few trees still standing in leaf. A solitary couple, a man and woman, plastic bags in hand, with a child in a buggy, are making their way as if returning from market. But in that bleak setting there is nothing else alive or moving. Set beside this chilling scene, the poems of a Dave Smith may appear as an extreme of frivolity. Anthony Hecht's assembly of poems on Death are rather like a deck of playing cards, skillfully made to be sure, but the death and devastation revealed in this picture are another matter altogether. And one thinks: Might this one day be Peoria, Trenton, or Denver? In our shifting and volatile world it seems a not unlikely possibility. And where then will our poets be?

The poems of Yehuda Amichai are proof that despite adversity, or perhaps because of it, a redeeming vitality is latent in the dialogue between society and the poet. In our case at present one half of that dialogue is largely missing.

Poetry Chronicle IV

One of the melancholy facts of late literary life is the periodic dying off of one's contemporaries, poets of one's own generation or older, and sometimes younger. The death late last year of Denise Levertov was such an instance, and there have been others in the past half decade. Meanwhile, the growing numbers of books by younger talents, a few of whom may one day prove to be an adequate replacement for our losses.

A handsome new Graywolf Press edition of William Stafford's poems* affords us a fresh look at one of the major figures of our time. Is there another American poet in whose work one can find, if at times half disguised, so much of contemporary history and events? In whose poems so much, both familiar and strange, is reflected, and all in that calm, neighborhood voice of his. When he says "we," as he often does, you know he means it.

> Mine was a Midwest home—you can keep your world.
> Plain black hats rode the thoughts that made our code.

---

*William Stafford, *The Way It Is: New and Selected Poems*, (St. Paul: Graywolf, 1998).

We sang hymns in the house; the roof was never God.
("Our Home")

A poetry so offhand at times, you think it might have been written by almost anyone. And then one realizes that no one else could have written so wisely and convincingly of ordinary events, like returning to a town in which one grew up.

> When I came back I saw many sharp things;
> the wild hills coming to drink at the river,
> the church pondering its old meanings.
> I believe the hills won; I'm afraid
> the girl who used to sing in the choir
> broke into jagged purple glass.
("Back Home")

Many of the better known, anthologized poems, "Traveling Through the Dark," "At the Bomb-Testing Site," "The Epigraph Ending in And," "The Farm on the Great Plains," need not be quoted here. Rather, I would call attention to, among so many others, poems like "Back Home," "At Our House," "Things I Learned Last Week"; that unusual poem, "Judgments," with its repeated phrase, "I accuse . . ."; and still another haunting piece, "New Letters to Thomas Jefferson," a prose poem written as a sequence of four letters addressed, apparently, to George Washington, and from which I quote the last:

My Old Friend,

   This morning the bees were swarming in the window well of the washroom. Birds were hunting each other. The root of the big yellow poplar was holding quiet as ever. Despite what we know and have done, I felt limited, alone. Across the morning light, particles were signaling what I cannot see.
As ever,
Thomas Jefferson

It is a tribute to Stafford's skill and inventiveness that—as the story goes—a Jefferson scholar who by some chance read this poem inquired of the poet where he had found the letters!

In Stafford's work we find an unfailing sense of time and place; we know where we are at this late end of the century. As Naomi Shihab Nye comments in her preface to this volume, "Rarely has a voice felt so intimate and so collective at once." Even when poems appear somewhat incidental to the best work, the supporting contribution is evident. And perhaps no other poet in our time has conveyed so consistent a sense of the American West and Midwest: "In scenery I like flat country. In life I don't like much to happen" ("Passing Remark"). A steadiness, braced with humor, as of someone poised to keep his balance in an uncertain world.

I last met with William Stafford at Ohio University's annual Literary Festival in the spring of 1993. He seemed at the time to be well and in his accustomed good spirits. In late August of that year I had a phone call from a friend that Stafford had died suddenly at his home in Oregon. And so the passing of another friend and fellow poet—of so unique a man and talent, rare in any age with his total absence of career politics and all related game playing; an integrity that informs the poems as well. From beginning to end, a steady devotion and accomplishment:

> No sound—a spell—on out
> where the wind went, our kite sent back
> its thrill along the string that
> sagged but sang and said, "I'm here!
> I'm here!" til broke somewhere,
> gone years ago, but sailed forever clear
> of earth. I hold—whatever tugs
> the other end—I hold that string.
>
> ("Father and Son")

To turn from Stafford's poems to the Polish poet Adam Zagajewski* is to depart from a familiar terrain and enter another space altogether, strangely removed from our still coherent neighborhoods:

> Europe is already sleeping, Night's animals,
> mournful and rapacious
> move in for the kill.
> Soon America will be sleeping too.
> > ("Houston, 6 p.m.")

I think I would know, without being told, that these lines were not written by an American. Indeed, it is hardly possible to find in this slim book a poem in which the history of our time is not in some way acknowledged. The events, the terrible absences, are there, even when not directly referred to.

> The train stopped at a little station
> and for a moment stood absolutely still.
> The doors slammed, gravel crunched underfoot,
> someone said goodbye forever,
> a glove dropped, the sun dimmed,
> the doors slammed again even louder,
> and the iron train set off slowly
> and vanished into the fog like the nineteenth century.
> > ("Iron Train")

If one has something to say, a few words will suffice. No thoughtful European writer today can entirely dismiss that inherited knowledge of camps and trains and exile—so lasting and searing an experience shared to a greater or lesser

---

*Adam Zagajewski, *Mysticism for Beginners*, (New York: Farrar, Staus, & Giroux, 1997).

degree by every nation on the continent. And this fact alone will distinguish the writing from its American counterpart. The difference can be said to lie in the fact that, in the present case, Zagajewski has this knowledge as part of himself; he doesn't have to invent it:

> You are my silent brethren,
> the dead,
> I won't forget you.

The one word, "refugees," calls up an image all too universal even now:

> and always that special slouch
> as if leaning toward another, better planet,
> with less ambitious generals,
> less snow, less wind, fewer cannons,
> less History (alas, there's no
> such planet, just that slouch).
>
> Shuffling their feet,
> they move slowly, very slowly,
> toward the country of nowhere
> and the city of no one
> on the river of never.
>
> ("Refugees")

Even a consideration of Dutch painting, with its allusions to some of the famous works of a classical period, cannot be made entirely free of our modern history:

> Doors were wide open, the wind was friendly.
> Brooms rested after work well done.
> Homes bared all. The painting of a land

without secret police.
Only on young Rembrandt's face
an early shadow fell. Why?
Tell us, Dutch painters, what will happen
when the apple is peeled, when the silk dims,
when all the colors grow cold.
Tell us what darkness is.

("Dutch Painters")

In an extended review of Zagajewski's work published in *The New Republic*, and in speaking of the often divided position of a writer in Poland today, the critic Adam Kirsch had this to say:

> The dilemma of solidarity and solitude is unfamiliar to an American, and it may be difficult for an American to enter into it fully. Here poetry is such a minor, sidelined pursuit that its practitioners by and large never even think of using their art to serve a larger cause . . . For some critics—George Steiner most egregiously—this amounts to a complacency that diminishes American Art. On this view, the moral crisis of Eastern Europe gives poetry an urgency and a public stature it can never have in the United States, where it is largely a hobby confined to writing workshops.

Kirsch's remarks appear to me consistent with that I have found in reading through well over twenty books for this review.

A typical modern exile, Zagajewski lives in Paris and teaches for part of the year at the University of Houston in Texas. This is the third of his books to appear in English, and the first I have read. Of the translations, and with no knowledge of the Polish language, I can only say that they appear to be faithful to the originals and result in poems that are moving and instructive in their own right.

This is otherwise a book to be taught by, in which a single stanza may hold, concentrated in a few words, more knowledge than is likely to be found in a year's subscription to your favorite newspaper or literary journal.

> Wisdom can't be found
> in music or fine paintings,
> in great deeds, courage,
> even love,
> but only in all these things,
> in earth and air, in pain and silence.
>   ("Shell")

To turn at this point to the American poet Frederick Feirstein* is to make yet another radical adjustment, and to enter a world largely removed from that painful history so clearly represented in the work of a contemporary Polish poet. The transition, rightly perceived, tells us something about our place as Americans in a world marked indelibly by events to which we have contributed while remaining at a sometimes thoughtful, sometimes indifferent distance.

Mr. Feirstein has received high praise from a number of his contemporaries. I have until now read little of his work other than that to be found in journals and anthologies. Often identified with the new formalist school, he writes primarily in traditional measures and in narrative, a neglected form that has in recent years been taken up by younger poets. Here is a sample passage:

> The past is like a library after dark
> Where we sit on the steps trading stories

Frederick Feirstein, New and Selected Poems, (Brownsville, Oreg.: Story Line Press, 1998).

With characters we imagined ourselves to be.
Neighbors in clothing from our childhood stroll by,
Unmolested, nodding at us, benevolently.
One with your father's face tips his fedora.
You lower your eyes in shame. I look back.
Someone is sitting at a long table,
Reading in the moonlight. I must look startled.
He holds a forefinger to his lips.
As if it is a candle for the dead.

("Manhattan Elegy")

The one-page narrative ends with these lines:

I walk to where the newsstand, shut,
Advertises brand names I'd forgotten.
I shove my hands into my pockets and whistle
A song we danced to when we were young.
I walk on for blocks, until I smell
Smoke from the burning borough of the Bronx.

"Manhattan Elegy" is part of a longer sequence of poems, a retelling of early life in New York, addressed to friends and written primarily in the present tense. Another poem in the sequence, "Song of the Suburbs," opens with these two stanzas:

The prospect of an automatic life:
Working from nine to five, dinner, then bed,
Maybe a night or two with the wife;
Watching T.V. or visiting the dead

Or fixing doorknobs or the sink on weekends.
That's what we rebelled against in youth.
We were going to fix the world, set social trends
In conscript dungarees. We possessed the truth.

There are also shorter poems that achieve a momentary intensity:

> To set aside rage
> And sit quietly at the water's edge
> At the edge of yourself
> And go past it
> And live in the body of the duck
> And the water lily
> And the crumbs of your own gift of bread.
>
> ("Edge")

And I would call attention to "Twentieth Century," vivid in its evocation of a vanished New York City: "A winter evening under a John Sloan El Fedoras tilt in unison against the wind."

"Family History," another narrative sequence, is engrossing in its characters, and with its irregular rhyming:

> How can I tell you, where do I begin?
> In Poland, a rich old man is asked to choose
> Between daughter and mother for his bride.
> He sighs, he shrugs, he strokes his whiskered chin.
> Shrewdly he takes a season to decide,
> There are no pogroms yet to rush the Jews.
>
> ....
>
> On my mother's side were Sam and Annie,
> Mild second cousins from the Russian Pale,
> Seemingly just my Jewish Gramps and Grannie
> Until, of cousre, I heard my uncle's tale.
> I loved my Grandma like the birds she fed.
> She spoke just a few English words, like, "Fred."

The individuals in the poems are often vivid and believable, a past recaptured in its telling. It is a world far removed from the one to be found in Zagajewski's poems, and by so much seems at times lacking in something essential to our age. To compare the two poets would perhaps be unfair: the one so expansive and American, the other haunted, concentrated on a history half obliterated. Nonetheless, there is an underlying criticism implied here, one that will have to be dealt with sooner or later.

Mr. Feirstein is a psychoanalyst in private practice in New York City. As such he must have abundant opportunity to observe people in their private lives as well as in their public behavior. To a considerable extent this is revealed and at times celebrated in his poems:

> Thus at Ratner's I began my history
> While ordering a travelogue of food:
> Cheese and blueberry blintzes, eggs, onions and lox,
> Kasha varnishkes, borscht, mushroom and barley soup –
> Enough to keep off thoughts of our mortality . . .
>
> ("Celebrating")

In his readable and intelligent book of essays on poetry, *One of the Dangerous Trades*,* Peter Davison writes of what he calls "The Refuge of the Present Tense." It is a failing all too evident in the majority of books I have considered for this review, and I am grateful to Mr. Davison for pointing it out so clearly. In the context he also remarks: "What of the poet's timeless roles: scribe, historian, cantor, prophet, musician, elegiast?" And he goes on to say:

> Today . . . our poets are not up to revolution. The status quo is too important to them. Not only their lives but their works, ignore the past, belittle the future . . . they stick to the things they know: the present, the visible limits of their lives, the

---

*Peter Davison, *One of the Dangerous Trades: Essays on the Work and Workings of Poetry*, (Ann Arbor: University of Michigan Press, 1991).

confines of their affairs. Even the tenses of their language reflect their commitment to the immediate present, to a world devoid of history.

Further consideration of Davison's words brings me to the poems of Thomas McGrath, who died in 1990 and whose world is by no means devoid of history. In his *Selected Poems, 1938 -1988*, also published by Copper Canyon Press, I turn to his "Elegy for the American Dead in Asia," one of the true and moving poems of our time, and which ends with these lines:

> And the public mourners come: the politic tear
> Is cast in the Forum. But, in another year,
> We will mourn you, whose fossil courage fills
> The limestone histories: Brave: ignorant: amazed:
> Dead in the rice paddies, dead on the nameless hills.

Nothing finer has been written of American involvement in the Asian wars.

*Letter to an Imaginary Friend** is McGrath's major work, many years in the making. The first part of it was published in 1963, and the last of its four parts completed in 1985. Poets and critics as different as Amy Clampitt and Philip Levine have praised it. Part diary, part letter, part history and polemics, it is, as Sam Hamill in his preface has called it, "a grand work of memory and recovery." Not perhaps since William Carlos Williams and Ezra Pound has a poet undertaken so ongoing an epic and prevailed to the end.

The poem begins in the country of his birth, in North Dakota, and moves out into the wider world in his psychological and mythological journey, into the space of

---

Thomas McGrath, Letter to an Imaginary Friend, (Port Townsend, Wash.: Copper Canyon Press, 1997).

country, nation, politics, war, and what seems to be an always diverted homecoming—from the family farm of his boyhood, schoolyard, college, and labor, and all in a circular pattern. Early in the poem he writes of leaving home and family:

> How could I leave them?
> I took them with me, though I went alone
> Into the Christmas dark of the woods and down
> The whistling slope of the coulee, past the Indian graves
> Alive and flickering with the gopher light.
>
> (Part One)

The freshness of the language endures. Later, he writes from another place that is still the same place:

> Dream and despair: the journey around a wound . . .
> Circularity again, with nothing laid true in a straight line
> Nor square with the sailor star nor the fence of the north forty
> But turning, turning . . .
>   Dakota, New York, Europe, Dakota, again,
> Los Angeles Frisco Dakota New York, Los Angeles
> Turning and turning . . .
>   Outbound on the far night journey . . .
>
> (Part One)

And later still:

> too dark to say anything clearly, but not too dark
> To see . . .
>   one foot in early twilight, the other in snow,
> (Now failing away in the western sky where a fair star
> Is traveling our half-filled trail from the still, fair field –
> rare light!—trailing us home toward the farmhouse lamp)
>
> (Part Three)

McGrath's personal history is unusual among poets in our time: World War II veteran, Rhodes scholar, labor organizer, blacklisted for his socialist sympathies in the McCarthy era—a varied background that certainly fed the man and poet. When he speaks, as he often does, of the "companions" and "brothers," he is not using a figure of speech for effect; he means it, having lived himself in a time when men, and women, might indeed be brothers and companions in a rightful cause. Of course, this fact also set him apart from most of his tenured contemporaries (though once perhaps it might not have done so) and his reputation has to an extent suffered accordingly.

Within the context of this review, a considered comparison of the work of McGrath and Frederick Feirstein might be a worthy undertaking: two views of history, two ways of telling. And with the example of both McGrath and Zagajewski in mind, I would suggest once more our need for a poetry that can include political thought and the philosophy of political life. If poets cannot be teachers, they are merely entertainers and of passing importance.

                             Then, Night.

Night, first of the high, great fog: blown down
From the vast Siberias and freezing unknown lands
Of the fierce bear and blue shy fox.

                        Blown past our sleep
Into the ninety-mile wind, a shifting of space itself.

Night of the Army then: its paper snow: proper:
And its fog of number: cold: and its graceless mossy
Sleep, like wine in a stone ear.

                                 (Part One)

An epic in the tradition of Williams' *Paterson* and Pound's *Cantos*, the varying verse lines filled with action, with talk, memory, personal and family history, love, and news of the world. The underlying landscape remains that of the West and the High Plains, their snow and wind and spaces. But it is also the landscape of human pain and want, of injustice, of theft and oppression; a work also of humor and a kind of lyrical retaliation.

I do not feel comfortable in attempting to summarize in a brief review a work of this scope. Let me instead direct potential readers to Sam Hamill's preface, and to the supporting afterword by the editor Dale Jacobson. And I would suggest further that readers give this book and the other work by this poet their dedicated attention. If poetry still means anything in this media-haunted world, here is a place to begin.

Meanwhile, and with the man and poet in mind, I would close with this brief personal acknowledgment: "Dear Tom, rest easy, you are not forgotten."

1998

V

MEMOIRS

Wartime: A Late Memoir

Wartime for me began, not with my time of service in the navy, from 1943 to 1946, nor with the Japanese raid on Pearl Harbor in December 1941, but with the Sunday edition of a Los Angeles newspaper in the early 1930s, and a series of compelling photographs of the trench warfare of World War I. We were then living in Long Beach where my father, a navy officer, was stationed. At the age of eight or nine I was fascinated by the pictures of American, British, and German soldiers lying dead or wounded in the dirt and mud of a contested ground somewhere in France. As I sat there on the floor of our living room with the paper spread before me, I recall asking my father about them, of the conflict they were a part of, and where he had been at the time. I don't recall what he said to me, but I do remember that he gently took the paper from me as being unsuitable for a boy my age.

And then, in what seems now to have been a compressed sequence, and following a major California earthquake and another summer on Puget Sound, we moved back east once more to Washington and were living at the navy yard. We soon had news of the Spanish Civil War, with the weekly issues of *Life magazine*, its front-page photographs and intensely visual articles on that war. By then I was allowed to read as I wished, and in fact the news as it came to us by radio and the movie house newsreels was impossible to ignore, and occupied a good deal of the discussion between my father and mother, his fellow officers and their wives. I recall now within a brief time the German annexation of Austria, the Italian campaign in Ethiopia, and soon enough the ground war in France; the warship sinkings, and then the German air assault on Britain—all that was slowly drawing this country into a world conflict. There was also the ongoing war in China, with the unforgettable photographic record of events like the Japanese Rape of Nanking, and there was much else. It is possible, then, to say that I spent much of my childhood in the atmosphere of war—the constant presence of it, the impending probability of it.

While I was still very young I was for a while caught up with making and playing with model airplanes, chiefly the fighters and bombers of World War I, and I may have imagined myself as a pilot in some future conflict. There were, and especially in the military environment in which I grew up, those moments when the wars of our time intruded in such a way as to be unavoidable, and I suspect there was always in the background a sense that sooner or later we would be drawn into the growing conflict, and I as well as many of my boyhood friends would be compelled to serve in one of the armed forces. Life in the meantime went on in its daily and weekly course, with schools and playtime, as usual.

In the early summer of 1941 we left the navy yard and moved briefly to Bremerton, Washington, where my father joined the battleship *Maryland* as its executive officer. That summer was for me, at age seventeen, a matter of spending as much time as I could on the lakes and rivers of the nearby Olympic Peninsula, with the family car now available for my use. It was otherwise an intense and brooding summer, and the European war was never far from thought and discussion. I recall one early evening at our house when the family was gathered at the radio and we heard the news of the German invasion of Russia. My father was sitting on the floor of the room, close by the radio, in a very intense silence. And then, as the news moved on to other events, he shook his head and said, half to himself: "Well, Napoleon tried that, and it didn't work." It was one of those moments that for me defined the time in which we lived.

In August of that summer my father went with his ship to Hawaii, and my mother, my brother, and I moved south to San Diego, to Coronado, where we were to spend the next year and a half in an increasingly tense time, waiting and listening. Within three months came the Japanese raid on Pearl Harbor and our entrance into the Pacific War. I recall vividly the voice of President Roosevelt on the school loudspeaker, announcing the declaration of war. We had been called to a special class session to hear his address. There were in our class two Japanese American students, Sammy Takeshita, who was a schoolyard bully, and his younger brother, Akira. When the president's voice had ceased, the rest of our class turned to look at Sammy and Akira, sitting with their faces turned down to their desks as in a deep shame. Shortly afterward they and their families vanished from our town. We were not told of their fate; it was not spoken of, and we did not see them again.

In the sudden turmoil, with night blackouts imposed, and the possibility of a Japanese invasion of the Pacific coast, we had no immediate news of my father stationed with his ship at Pearl Harbor. There came a wire, and then a letter, telling us in graphic detail of the bombing and the fires, the sinking of the *Arizona* and other battleships, and the loss of some of his fellow officers; but he himself was safe, and his ship, the *Maryland*, had escaped with only minor damage.

Soon enough came the induction of eighteen-year-olds into the army, the marines, and the navy. We saw our classmates disappear into the training camps, shipped east or west to join one of the forces. Those of us not yet of age took advantage of the freedom we still had to party and drink on weekends and after school hours, making the most of the time remaining to us.

And then, early in January 1943, came my summons to report the navy enlistment office in San Diego. Of that experience I recall that it took place at night somewhere near the waterfront of the city. I had taken the ferry from Coronado and joined a long line of young men my age. What happened next was source of acute embarrassment for me. When very young I had a terrible fear of needles, of flu shots and blood tests. When it came my turn to step before the medic with my sleeve rolled up, I felt myself in a near faint, to be steadied momentarily by one of the men standing close to me. When the paperwork was done, I made my way back to the ferry and to Coronado. Soon after, my senior year unfinished, I had to leave school and report to the San Diego Naval Training Station where I spent the next several months, learning the drills, competing in company athletics—many things, in fact, that I disliked having to do.

One particularly unpleasant incident remains fixed in my mind. Our company drill sergeant, a pompous little man, one day lined us up in ranks and gave us a brief lecture on what was expected of us in the time to come. We listened to him tell us in a strutting tone that we were there to learn our duties, and then go out to join one of the battle fleets and "kill those little yellow bastards!" That was the message, and I think I was not the only member of my company to feel a certain real uneasiness on listening to that strident voice. Otherwise, I did well in my training, and when the period was over I received a commendation from our commanding officer.

At some point during that early period I had been assigned to a special training in underwater sound detection, or submarine detection as it was also called, and in a new technology known as radar, then in an early stage of development. The two disciplines were soon combined, and I became in a relatively short time what was then called a sonarman third class. It was a rank I kept throughout the war. I had no interest in advancement.

On completing the initial training I was sent north to San Pedro to join briefly a battleship crew. I have forgotten the reason for this move, but one event at the time stands clearly in mind. It was a Sunday morning in early summer, and a Catholic Mass was announced aboard ship. I had until then been a steady and believing churchgoer having been raised in the Church, and at one time considered joining one of the orders, becoming a priest. I was sitting alone that morning on the main deck under one of the large guns of the ship. For reasons unclear to me, I made what turned out to be a major decision: I would not go to Mass that morning. Whether during the wartime that followed I remained with that decision I cannot say, but I recall at that moment a very deep sense of pain and guilt, a loneliness I had not felt before.

Soon after, I was shipped east with two of my mates from the training station. We went by train to Chicago, where we stopped for a day and a night, and where one of my friends had family. From there we went our separate ways to the ships and stations that awaited us. I went south to Norfolk, Virginia, to join temporarily a new sub chaser, a small surface vessel destined to be turned over to the Cuban navy, as we were told. What I mainly recall of that brief duty is the terrible summer heat on the edge of the Dismal Swamp, and the confined and sweating space below deck. Our small crew with its captain soon set out, bound south to Miami. Along the way we were to be on watch for German submarines rumored to be scouting the Atlantic coast. I spent the better part of my time below deck, listening on the sound gear. We did not encounter any U-boats.

At the end of that brief voyage we left the chaser in the Miami harbor and were housed overnight in a downtown hotel.

Of that summer evening I remember looking out the hotel window on the city skyline and the harbor beyond, feeling some keen regret on having to leave our ship behind. I was soon back on a train, sent north to Boston. My mother and father had moved to Washington during this time, and It had been arranged for me to stop there for a brief visit. My parents occupied an apartment in the northwest part of the city at an address I can no longer recall, and of that visit I remember very little. It was a melancholy time in many respects, with the war gaining in scope and intensity. I did not want to be shipped out to the Pacific, and I also missed many of my high school friends. I had no certainty as to where my navy service might end, and of the war itself no end was in sight.

One incident in that brief Washington visit remains clear. There was a piano in the apartment, and with little else to occupy me, and much to the surprise of myself and my parents, I sat down at the piano one afternoon and began to play, making up the tune, the chords, and the melody. I may have had some early introduction to the piano, now long forgotten, but surely I had no trained skill in playing. Yet I sat there, making for myself a provisional composition, as my mother looked on in quiet amazement.

And then I was once more on the train, on my way to Boston to join a newly commissioned destroyer, the USS *Knapp*, DD 653, with a crew of three hundred men of whom I knew not one, most of them no more experienced in warfare than I was. I took an assigned bunk below deck, and in the days that followed I was introduced to the workings of the ship: to the submarine detection room and equipment far below, and to the radar station in a room behind the wheel deck, where I would spend the better part of my time in the months to come.

During this time I met with an old navy yard friend and neighbor, Ginna Adell, who was then living in Boston with her parents and with whom I had had an odd and affectionate relation. We met during the one brief shore leave I had, but of that meeting I recall only a phone call between us, and then our standing together on the dock below my ship, saying goodbye to each other in a moment of sadness. The next day my ship left Boston Harbor, bound south to Panama and the Canal Zone that would take us out to the Pacific and into major combat.

In company with another destroyer we stopped briefly off the coast of Cuba, at Guantanamo Bay. There had been a shipboard rumor that we might be allowed to go ashore for a short break, but instead we raised anchor and turned west toward Panama and were soon passing through the canal on our way to the Pacific. I had hoped at some point to go ashore with some of my shipmates and make an evening tour of the local Panama City bars; but I was assigned duty on the shore patrol. I was given some special uniform identify, with a club or a nightstick, and with one other of my shipmates instructed to make the drunks returning to the ship that evening behave themselves, using force only If absolutely necessary. I can recall but one incident that evening: an encounter with a burly and drunken seaman, unknown to me and whom I tried to put under temporary arrest. But he was far more than I could handle, and my efforts were fairly futile until help arrived. I learned that I was not cut out to be a policeman; I disliked having to use force, and I was at that age far too shy to make the needed impression on an older and more aggressive sailor.

Leaving the canal behind us, we sailed out into the Pacific, north along the Mexican coastline, to stop briefly offshore at San Diego. Looking toward that familiar coast, I wanted badly to go ashore and see my mother who had moved back to Coronado and was living alone, with my father, myself, and now my brother, Bob, all in uniform and on our way to the battle zone far west.

Our ship turned west toward Hawaii, and in a few days without incident, very much on the alert, we were docked at

Pearl Harbor. We were all given a final shore leave, and I and some of my mates took a bus or cab into Honolulu, where we toured the bars, becoming in some cases thoroughly drunk. I recall waking from a long nap under a banana tree in a city park at midnight, roused by the flashing lights and traffic noise; but that is all I remember. We returned to our ship by early morning, and were soon bound out into the war zone to join Task Force 58, one of the major fleets, made up of aircraft carriers, battleships and cruisers, tankers and supply ships. Destroyers like the *Knapp* were stationed on the outer edge of the fleet, on picket duty, to listen for enemy submarines, watch for aircraft, and guard the larger and more vulnerable main fleet.

While en route to the south central Pacific and our first major engagement with an enemy force, we experienced one of the most disturbing episodes of the war. This was what was called the "Shellback Initiation," an ancient rite performed on those who had not previously crossed the Equator or the International Date Line. We had heard rumors of this, of the sometimes brutal and scary things that would be imposed on the initiates, and in spite of the proximity of enemy forces. When the day came, a shipboard interval was declared, and the older, more experienced crew members forced us to line up and be subjected to a series of humiliating procedures: to eat and drink disgusting items cooked up for the occasion; to shed some or all of our clothing and be whipped from behind as we filed through a line of laughing and cheering sailors; painted with foul-smelling greases, and to be lavished with additional humiliations throughout the day. Much of this is long since lost to memory; what I most recall is the fearful anticipation of it, and then the sense of relief and escape to our showers and bunks below decks. It was soon over, and, having recovered, we were welcomed among the veterans as true seamen.

Of the many engagements that followed, the names and locations are mixed in memory and in no certain sequence. We were present at the Marshall Islands invasion, took part in a bombardment of Kwajalein, and participated in the major battle of Truk, an island stronghold of Japanese forces. There were many prolonged maneuvers and battles among the atolls and islands of the south central Pacific. At one point in the long months ahead we were sent down into the East Indies, to Espiritu Santo, in what was called a "screening" operation to protect aircraft carriers in the area. Of that brief episode I recall glimpses of the dense tropical vegetation on the islands we drew close to, but mainly a terrible unrelenting heat that made sleeping below decks nearly impossible. And then, in a short time, we were headed north again to join our major task force. There followed, from month to month, our participation in the assault on the Marianas, Saipan and Tinian, and then the Philippines, intense and lengthy engagements in which we were placed on continuous watch to support the invasion forces sent ashore to secure the islands from the enemy. The ground war was often prolonged and difficult. I remember the shellfire, the night watches, the alerts at any moment, when everything else was abandoned and we ran to our battle stations, prepared at any moment for the anticipated command: "Hard right rudder!" "Full speed ahead!" "Ready: Fire at will!" And there was also the constant alertness required for possible submarines and aircraft, the occasional unloading of a depth charge when contact with an enemy submarine had been confirmed, or so we assumed, for we could seldom be certain. Only once did some debris float to the surface in our ship's wake to confirm that we had struck an enemy craft far below us.

My battle station shifted back and forth between the radar screen on the bridge deck and the underwater sound room below, with an occasional turn at the helm, helping to steer the ship under the guidance of one of the officers. On a relatively small ship like a destroyer many of us were conditioned to take part in various shipboard duties, to be of help when needed. There were days, sometimes weeks, between engagements, when we had time to refuel from one of the tankers in the fleet, and to replace the ship stores that enabled the crew to have a decent meal two or three times a day.

Once, during a long separation from the supply vessels, we ran out of most standard foodstuffs, and a typical meal might consist of a badly cooked cereal, or perhaps a slice of stale bread and a few crackers; but no coffee or milk, nothing fresh in the way of fruit or meat. During one noontime meal I discovered in my bowl of wheat cereal what I thought were some grains of rise; and then I realized that those small grains were in fact weevil maggots that had infested the flour and cereals stored too long in that dense tropical heat. Sickened, I rose from the table, dumped my ration in the garbage, and went without a meal that day.

And then came the day of refueling and taking on supplies. Our ship was secured to the side of one of the supply ships, and we all went to work carrying aboard sacks of rice and flour, cartons of canned milk, fresh fruits, meat and vegetables—all that we had run out of during the many weeks of patrol on the edge of the task force. In spite of the ever-present threat of enemy action, we had for a few hours a kind of shipboard party; and having finally fed, we felt ready once more to face the war.

Wartime was not always an unrelenting sequence of actual warfare. Between battle alerts and routine duties, my shipmates and I often played cards, or we discussed the books we had read or were reading, and otherwise we talked about our lives, our families, what we planned to do when the war was over and we were returned to that civilian life we had left behind. There was a small library available, replenished from time to time by an exchange with one of the other ships, and among the books were some that we passed among us, to be read and handed on to the next reader. We read *Gone With The Wind*, and there was a trilogy by the Chicago writer James T. Farrell, *Studs Lonigan*. Among our small group of sonarmen and others on the bridge crew were two or three from the Chicago area, one reason perhaps that we all turned to the Studs Lonigan story. Having read the novels or at least a substantial part of them, we would sit in one of our confined spaces and discuss the story and the characters, what we liked about them and so forth. Though among us at the time there were no college graduates, I remember our discussions as being sensitive and intelligent, and perhaps more so than a similar group of mainly working-class individuals might be capable of today.

Another related break in routine occurred when we were given a recording of the Broadway musical *Oklahoma*, recently premiered in New York. I think we were captivated by the music in that work, by the songs that took us back to the home country we had left behind. I remember moments when we sang to ourselves and to each other some of the main chorus, and we were once joined in this by one of the officers on deck at the time. It was exciting, and in ways that must have reminded many of us of our lost school days.

In the enforced isolation of weeks and months of sea duty, with the mail sporadic, introspection was not uncommon among us. It was one of the compensations that prolonged danger and social isolation can sometimes bestow on individuals, whether alone or with comrades. The names of my shipmates are long forgotten, but in what remains to me of my memory of the period, I recall a perspective not easily acquired in more ordinary times.

My shipmates and I did not indulge in any patriotic display. We were there to do a job, to perform in a necessary situation as best we could—not one we had chosen, but which had been imposed on us by circumstances or simply by fate. Nor did we at any time display a hatred of our enemy the Japanese. Individually at least, they were not there to be destroyed, but were a people who for one reason or another were "on the other side" and perhaps no more inclined to war than we were. I remember when we rescued three Japanese crew members from a sunken submarine, and we kept them on board briefly before transferring them to another ship. They were confined below decks, and were quiet and obedient. We fed them and were kind to them, understanding that we might have found ourselves in a similar situation at any time during the long conflict.

One major event of the war was only indirectly the result of enemy action. In late December of 1944 a large part of our fleet was sent into the South China Sea. This turned out to be a serious miscalculation on the part of our fleet commander. Our destroyers were by then low on fuel, and we were scheduled to meet with the fleet tankers and refuel. At this time an immense tropical storm, a typhoon, appeared, apparently unpredicted, and plunged us into a major crisis. Loss of fuel meant also a loss of sufficient ballast, and smaller ships like destroyers were in immediate danger from the enormous wind-driven seas that swept over us. What I recall most vividly is the continual shuddering and shaking of our ship, with the decks awash and the impossibility of going out onto an open deck in any safety.

During the worst of this I was at my station on the bridge where I and others of the crew watched an instrument, the inclinometer, swing from side to side as the ship rolled heavily to port or starboard, to hang there briefly and swing back again. Bundled in our life jackets, we all held fast to any means of support, knowing that at any moment our ship might not recover stability and would simply roll over and sink. It was at this time impossible to have a meal served in the mess hall. Dishes and cookware went sliding from the counters and tables, the food spilled and wasted.

We made one attempt to secure alongside one of the

tankers, but it proved to be impossible to maintain the fuel lines. With the extreme rolling and pitching of our ship and the larger tanker, the hoses broke apart, spewing the black oil into the air and into the boiling seas. We were forced to pull away and attempt to regain our position in the fleet.

In the midst of all this turmoil we learned of the loss of three destroyers in our fleet that had capsized in the ocean. We ourselves rescued two crew members from one of the ships, but I no longer remember the details of that rescue. Soaked and exhausted as we were, we finally emerged from the storm and were able to refuel. We had by then confirmation of what was later described as the worst naval event of the Pacific War, with the loss of over nine hundred men.

After nearly thirteen months of warfare, with one serious engagement following on another, our ship was in need of repairs and a general overhaul. In late January 1945 w were ordered back to the States, to the San Pedro Naval Station and a period of leave for officers and crew. En route we were given a day and an evening in Honolulu, a wonderful break from shipboard routine: beer and whiskey, music, and for some of us, available women. I remember only a smoky bar, a few empty stools, and a glass in my hand.

In February we docked at San Pedro and stepped ashore for a substantial period. I took my leave to go south to Coronado and spend time with my mother and with any schoolmates who might still be there. It was a drastically changed world by then, and I found myself mostly alone without companions in the small town from which I had entered the service. Alone as she was then, in order to remain active and contribute something to the war effort, my mother had joined the Red Cross Ambulance Service, and had learned to look after the vehicles and take part in caring for some of the wounded servicemen brought in from the Pacific conflict.

One of my high school friends, Beverly Bogue, was still

in town. She was nominally engaged, I understood, to another classmate who was also in the service and whose name I have forgotten. She and I met one evening to see a movie at the downtown Coronado theater. Along with the feature film we watched a newsreel sequence of current events in the war and in national life. President Roosevelt was shown briefly in conference somewhere in Europe, perhaps in Tehran or Yalta with other Allied leaders, Winston Churchill among them. Beverly and I were sitting close, and at one moment she leaned toward me and whispered of Roosevelt: "He looks tired." And he did. FDR was someone who for many of us was more like a close friend than a national leader.

Not long afterwards Beverly and I borrowed my mother's car and drove down to Tijuana, Mexico, where we spent part of the day walking some of the crowded streets. We then drove on farther south to Rosarito Beach. We spent the night in a hotel, and much of the following day on the nearby ocean beach, enjoying the sun, relaxing in a close and friendly way. What we talked about I cannot remember, but it was one of the very few wartime periods when I felt something of that closeness we associate with romance.

And then the leave was over. I said good-bye to my mother and returned to San Pedro to join my shipmates for another long episode of war. When I think back on it, I remember that the mood of things was deeply pessimistic at the time, and none of us wanted to go back out into what was an increasingly deadly combat, with the battle of Okinawa already looming or in progress, and no end of it in sight. Many of the crew had been drinking heavily when they boarded the *Knapp*; I learned from one of my mates that our captain himself had been carried aboard drunk the night before we were to leave. It was in fact a deeply melancholy moment in that wartime life, and understandably so for most of us whose lives had been seriously interrupted and placed in jeopardy.

We stopped once more at Pearl Harbor, but were allowed no leave this time. Things were growing more and more serious out in the battle zone, and our ship and crew as well as others now returning from the West Coast were urgently needed. Our arrival at Okinawa occurred in the midst of one of the worst battles of the Pacific War. We sailed into a harbor on the main island to see so many damaged and half-sunken ships, some of which were upended in the dark evening water of the harbor. It was, as I remarked at the time, like entering a graveyard, made all the more devastating because several of the badly damaged or sunken ships had accompanied us in previous engagements.

Our destroyers were placed on picket duty, patrolling the coastline and the waters outside the island. We were to intercept the suicide planes that flew down nightly from Japan to plunge into and destroy any American vessel they encountered. Our nights were nearly sleepless. All was in darkness aboard ship; our eyes were focused on the flashes and signals of the radar screen and, when possible, on what could be seen of land and horizon in the darkness. It was a ghostly, almost surreal period in its nighttime silence, its inherent mystery and uncertainty. Only once were we directly menaced when, in what was then daylight, one of the suicide bombers, perhaps damaged by aircraft fire, soared over our ship and plunged into the sea. It was close, and many ships of our fleet were not so lucky.

In those closing weeks of the war the action went on, with bombing raids on the enemy-held islands north of Okinawa becoming more frequent. We were preparing for an invasion of the Japanese mainland and what we presumed would be a prolonged land war. And then, sometime in August of that final year, we heard on the ship's radio the announcement of a new weapon, a bomb that had been dropped on one of the Japanese cities, with terrible results. We did not know at the time what this new weapon was, not having been told in any way about its use. But we all sensed at that moment that something unprecedented had occurred; and we responded if only for a moment with deep silence. The war would soon be over, though we were not certain of this until the Japanese surrender was announced some time later. Meanwhile our night alerts and daytime patrols continued.

The formal surrender took place in Tokyo Bay on September 2, amid a vast assembly of American and British warships. We were anchored not far from the battleship *Missouri* on which the official surrender was held. I recall a deep calm among us. Finally after so many months and years, the war was over, and we would soon be home to begin our lives where we had left them in what seemed at times to have been another world. At a special gathering on the main deck our commanding officers expressed their gratitude for our service, but I do not recall any shipboard celebration. There was among us mainly a sense of relief, of a difficult assignment completed.

Following the surrender, and for several weeks thereafter, we were assigned with other destroyers to a patrol of the Japanese coast, one of the closing maneuvers of the war. We sailed to the north end of the main island of Honshu, and turned south again, remaining at times at anchor offshore, on guard for any attacks by the former enemy. And then, in late November, in the company of one or two other ships, we returned to Pearl Harbor. For a few days we were allowed leave once more, and I was able to spend some time with my father, now a captain, who was there also, briefly ashore from his ship and winding up his sea duties. He had met the captain of my ship, the *Knapp*, who had told him of my good behavior, of my calmness under fire, of my being an example to my shipmates. I was, naturally, pleased to hear this, unexpected though it was.

In thinking about it later, I recalled a moment in one of our most intense battle situations. I was bent over the radar screen attempting to track an enemy ship or aircraft, when the deck officer looked at me with a critical eye and remarked, "You're really enjoying this, aren't you?"—as if I were in some way violating official protocol. I remember standing up from the screen and replying with a smile: "Yes, sir . . . I am!" And in fact I was, in a certain acute sense, revitalized by the excitement of that combat, a welcome relief from the long days and nights of boredom, no action, but hours spent looking and listening, waiting for something to happen.

Our crew left Pearl Harbor and arrived at San Pedro in late December of 1945. Our discharge proceedings went smoothly, and in early January I was back in civilian life, my uniform laid aside and my discharge papers in order, with a further commendation from one of our officers, a medal and citation. I left with a certain pride that it was in fact over, and we had won the war.

Shortly after the discharge proceedings, having said good-bye to the shipmates I had come to know, I returned to Coronado with one of my friends whose name I no longer remember, and who would soon be headed home to Ohio. We spent a day and a night at the old oceanfront Hotel Del while coming to terms with civilian life, experiencing a strange and peaceful atmosphere. My mother had by then moved back to Washington with my father, and they expected me to join them there and decide on further schooling and on what course my life might take now that the war was over. I had no definite plans, but at some point during the war I had begun drawing with pen and ink, working with watercolors, and it seemed I might enter art school once things had settled down. But all of this was still vague, and of the future in general I was still uncertain.

I spent my remaining days in Coronado visiting with a few of my old classmates recently returned from service. We faced the saddening fact that some of the friends we shared would not come back; we recalled their names, wondering where they had died, where they might be buried. Had I not been able to join the navy I too might have ended up on one of the beaches with an invasion force, a casualty, and never returned from the war. I owed my good fortune to my father who had obtained a waiver for me and arranged for me to join the navy, not the army to which I was initially headed.

In those final days in Coronado there were a number of parties, or "open houses" as they were called. I remember one evening in which a large number of us, schoolmates and girlfriends, spilled out into the street in front of one of the houses, openly drinking to the accompaniment of loud music. We were, however briefly, a rowdy and celebratory crew, but the police understood and left us alone.

In mid-January I took the train east to Washington, with a brief stop in Chicago as was the custom then. I joined my family at their house on Windom Place close to the District line, and slowly began to accustom myself to a new life as civilian and potential student of art. My brother, Bob, still in uniform, soon left to finish up his service at a Great Lakes station.

Many postwar tensions were prominent in the news, but they were not now the important events in my life. Had I joined the U.S. Naval Reserve as we were encouraged to do, I might have been recalled to active duty in 1950 and sent out to the Korean conflict. But I had refused the offer; those three years at sea had been enough for me, and I had another life to begin and had to somehow find my way.

In thinking about that war and my own experience of it, I have come to feel that there is at least one important lesson to be learned: that there are certain things about oneself, one's character, and about humanity in general, that one may never know until one has been, if only for a brief time, in mortal danger—at extreme risk, physically and psychologically, and in which one's very existence is in doubt. There are no rules for this, and for the individual at times it may very well prove otherwise than I have stated here. But in that situation of mortal risk there can be a momentary focus of energy and attention, the like of which might for some be found in intellectual life, and which I feel to be, in certain important respects, a fundamental fact of our earthly life.

I have known extreme danger at other times—in the wilderness, in a major earthquake, or a car wreck—moments when one's life may be in peril and for a prolonged period. But at this distance I can assess and value for what it was worth that period of wartime and the lessons it had to teach. I can wish that it will never happen again, but I understand at the same time that some historical moment may once again bring us to that brink from which only keen attention to the task at hand, good fortune, and something else not easily defined, can rescue us. Perhaps there is no long-term rescue for humanity from the terror of war, rapine, murder, and destruction. A prevailing peace on this earth may never occur, but that does not relieve us of the attempt to make it possible.

In the patriotic fervor of this present moment it may be good and useful to recall those episodes of a past war, how it happened, what it meant to us at the time, and what, if anything, we gained from it aside from new means of death and destruction. A few years ago, in response to a review of a book on war in the *New York Times*, I wrote a letter to the editor of the paper, the conclusion of which is as follows:

> Considering the nature of warfare in our time, World War II was the last major conflict from which any nation or people might conceivably emerge victorious. Given the world we now share, and the nature of the weapons created and made available, no military victory, in the historical sense of this, can be possible. How we resolve, or fail to resolve, the tensions in this predicament, seems certain to determine the future of humanity on this planet.

Looking back now on a major war in which I took part, I can only reaffirm the conviction as stated in this brief quotation. The question we face is whether a sufficient number of us, citizens and statesmen, can admit the truth of it and act accordingly.

1995

On the Street

I have never been a street person, someone for whom the
street, the doorway, the alley corner, is home for a prolonged
period. During my early days in Fairbanks in the summer
of 1947, I often slept in the back of a truck I owned while
parked downtown on Second Avenue, waking at times to the
sound of traffic, to closing doors, and to voices on the street
in the long summer twilight. Then too I often camped by the
roadside outside of town, with a makeshift tent set up, and a
small woodstove, while I searched the nearby country for that
piece of land I had come to find and settle.

And there was a day in August during that first summer
when, no longer with a car or truck of my own, I walked nearly
thirty miles from my campsite at Richardson toward Fairbanks
before I finally caught a ride. I stopped briefly for coffee at one
of the roadhouses where I approached an older couple on their
way into town and asked them for a ride. They took a quick,
sideways look at my rough clothing, my probably unshaven
face, and refused me. In the long, footsore hours that followed
I felt at times like an itinerant hobo on the road to nowhere.
An occasional incident like this, however, was something I took
in stride as being in the nature of things at the time, part of the
adventure I had set out on in that early postwar period.

But once or twice in my life at a later time I came close enough to understand something of that state of things, of utter homelessness: nowhere to go, no means of getting there. In late August of 1948, when I had returned to Washington from my first year and a half in Alaska and was reentering school to continue my art studies, I rented a small top-floor room on N Street, not far from Connecticut Avenue. In the dense later summer heat it was difficult to sleep in that room, and for a night or two I took my blanket and a pillow and went into the park area on Dupont Circle to spend the night in what breeze there was at the time, and as I had recently seen others do. The streets were safe then as they are not now, and I found myself in a kind of neighborhood of like-minded people: men, women, and children, most of whom had homes to go to, but in those days before air-conditioning they were drawn out into the fresh air of the open park. Some were sleeping on the benches, others on the grass, and many of them engaged in conversation until late in the evening. I remember talking with a couple of friendly older men about my recent venture to the far north and what I had done there.

The days and nights gradually cooled, and I was soon taken up with school, with classes and studio work at American University, and no longer needed to sleep in the park. My situation then was not dire, though I was poor enough with my GI allowance, barely able to pay the monthly rent of $25, to buy my meals and art supplies, and an occasional book. To be poor, as a student, as an artist, was at the time very much in the bohemian tradition, and I was not alone in my circumstance.

In early January of 1950, having finished a year of study in painting and sculpture at American University, and a period of work as a draftsman at the Navy Department, I moved to New York to continue my art studies. I was immediately and radically introduced to the Lower East Side of Manhattan, to the Bowery under the Third Avenue El, and to a poverty encountered daily on my walks to Hans Hofmann's School on Eighth Street in the Village. This was still at the time a neighborhood where the handcarts and horse wagons were common on nearby Rivington Street, with the block-long City Market flourishing not far away on Houston Street—a New York long since vanished.

It was during those first weeks in New York that I became aware of the worst of that homelessness: the men, and sometimes the women, camped by a blazing trash can, with the elevated train rumbling overhead, their hands held out for anything you might be willing to give, whether a coin or a slice of bread. My fellow student and roommate, Felix, who had moved to New York from Washington two years previously, knew better than I how to push them aside, and in truth we had nothing to give them. I was appalled, not having seen anything like it in my relatively safe and harbored childhood, though I had glimpsed as a boy, in the 1930s, the unemployed men and women in southeast Washington, staring from the steps of run-down houses as we drove by. And I had, more recently, seen a war from the decks of a navy destroyer in the south-central pacific, and had taken part in many major engagements, but had seen few dead and no prisoners. As difficult as it had been in some respects, with the imminent threat from enemy submarines, from bombs and suicide planes, I had a bunk to sleep in and a meal, morning and evening. The street, and all that it implied, was far off.

In late spring of that year I and a few of my fellow students decided that we would save our money and camp in tents on the dunes outside Provincetown where Hofmann's school was to move for the summer. For some reason, perhaps because I had by then some money saved in a small bank account, and because my homesteading venture in Alaska gave the impression of my having had some needed experience, I found myself chosen to go out to the Cape early in order to sort out the situation and see what might be done, what we would need, and who we might turn to for help if we should need it.

Sometime in April, then, I took the train and the bus from New York to Provincetown. I made the serious mistake of not taking enough money with me, assuming I might go to a local bank and cash a check. When I arrived in Provincetown I found that I had spent nearly all my pocket money on bus and train fare. I went to a downtown bank, only to find that they would not accept my check, the lady behind the counter looking at me as if I were some kind of New York crook, or simply a drifter. I had not eaten that day since leaving New York, but was able to buy a cup of coffee at a café near the waterfront run by two Greek brothers, and to whom I explained my situation. Meanwhile, I had gone to the Chamber of Commerce at the town wharf, and had sent a wire to my bank; but I would have to wait until the following day for the money to arrive. Where was I to spend the night that was soon to come?

I went to a local rooming house suggested to me by the café owners. I explained my problem to the landlady standing warily at the head of a steep stairway, and asked if I might have a room for the night; I would pay her the following day. No, she would not allow me a room. I then went to a nearby church and asked the priest for some help, a bed for the night. Again, I found no welcome. Night was coming on, it was chilly in the April dark. I returned to the café, where the Greek brothers gave me a meal, something to stay the hunger pangs. I was nearly twenty-six years old, already used to some hardships, but not until then had I faced a night on the street alone.

I walked Commercial Street, the main waterfront thoroughfare, searching and wondering. Finally I found an enclosed doorway in what appeared to be a vacant building. I had nothing with me but a light jacket and a small handbag, not having expected I might need bedding or a change of clothing. I curled up on the doorway out of sight of anyone walking the nearby street, and with my small bag for a pillow, managed a fitful, shivering slumber for some hours. It was then past midnight; I had stayed in the café until closing time, if only to keep warm. More than once during that night I got to my feet in the small rough space, moved my arms and legs to warm the, and lay down again in the dark. I could smell the wet salt air mixed with the sour dampness of the wood floor I was lying on; intermittently a fog horn pierced the darkness. Toward morning I became aware of the town fishermen on their way to the boats, their voices coming to me as if in sleep, their boots grating on the rough stone of the street. I slept again; it would be some time yet before the café opened.

And then day came. I had coffee and something to eat at the café close by, while I waited for my money to be wired from New York. And sometime later that morning it arrived. I paid the Greek brothers and thanked them for their kindness. And then, feeling that I had failed in what I had set out to do, I took the bus and the train back to Hartford and New York. I arrived late at the flat I shared on Stanton Street with my friend Felix and his wife; with some pained embarrassment I explained to them what had happened. It was a lesson, one I did not need to repeat.

After a summer spent tenting on the dunes with a small group of my fellow students, mostly afoot, walking the two or three miles into town (another but healthier version of the street), I rented a small cottage in Provincetown and devoted some quiet weeks to writing and walking the empty beaches. I returned to New York in November, and to our shared apartment. By then it had become obvious that the place was too small for the three of us, and I would have to find another space for myself.

Searching halfheartedly through the neighborhood, for the city was still scary and strange to me, I found a room in a run-down building a few blocks up Stanton Street, and moved in with my typewriter and the rest of my scarce belongings. I paid $20 a month for that room, hardly bigger than a closet. So far as I could tell, the building was occupied by impoverished immigrants, and I listened until late at night to the conversation in Spanish of a couple in the room next to mine.

I soon discovered that the room was infested with cockroaches, with bedbugs, fleas, and mice. I had not slept there long before I found myself itching and scratching, bitten from head to foot by the bugs I found impossible to rid myself of, and despite the insect powders and sprays I made use of— whatever was available at the time. I came to school one day, depressed, my face and neck spotted with red welts. A friend, the painter Franz Kline, stopped me on the stairway to the Hofmann studio and asked what had happened to me. I told him, and he said, in an urgent voice I can still recall: "John! Move out!" But it was not so easily done.

I spent no more time in that room than was necessary in order to sleep and be out of the weather. Between sessions at school I worked at my poems, using a chair as a prop for my typewriter, all the while watching for the bugs. Finally, however, after a few short weeks, I had to get out, as nothing seemed to relieve me of the pests in the bedding and woodwork. The enforced isolation had become oppressive, and my depression over it was increasing.

Three young women students at Hofmann's, whom I had met in Provincetown, rented a loft not far from the building where I was camping. Learning of my situation, they invited me to dinner one evening. I had by then decided to leave my infested room, but doing so threatened to put me on the street, as there was nowhere I could afford to move to. Later that evening, with a blanket and pillow loaned to me by my friends, I went down to the East River at the foot of Stanton Street, found a bench by the water, and resolved to spend the night.

I slept uneasily, awakened from time to time by a boat on the river, by traffic on the street above, by voices in the near distance. It was by then deep winter, and chilly on that open bench. Sometime after midnight I awoke to a light shining in my face. I sat up, alarmed, to find two police officers on patrol who had seen me there and stopped to ask if I was all right. A little shaken by the encounter, I explained my situation, told them that it was only temporary, that I did not intend to remain there. Satisfied that I was not ill or in danger, the officers wished me a good night and left.

I went back to sleep. It is in some odd way a tribute to the state of things in those days that even in so run-down a part of New York I was in no apparent danger of being robbed or molested. Today it might be a very different story.

The night passed. I awoke in the morning, gathered my blanket and pillow, and, stiff and sore from a night on that hard bench, I went to find some breakfast. Not long after that, my women friends, Jo, Louise, and Peggy, agreed that I could share their loft, which was large, until I found something else. No more bugs, no more nights on the street or the threat of that. I had found a haven, and good company.

Early the following year, Peggy and I were married at the Manhattan Courthouse, and moved from Stanton Street to a small apartment near Third Avenue. There too we were reminded of the nearby lurking poverty: men sleeping in the doorway to our building, the never-ending coal soot on the windowsill, the occasional bug in our bedding, and like a deep underground menace, the shaking rumble of the elevated train night and day.

Years later I read George Orwell's *Down and Out in London and Paris* and understood something of a kind of brotherhood among the less fortunate in our sometimes too comfortable world. The street is still there, still home to the many thousands who do not share in our temporary wealth, ease, and convenience. One may view these people as a nuisance to be swept aside, or as a kind of conscience, half visible but never entirely hidden—a haunting of a condition that may yet return.

As I write these words, I think of the Washington Metro stations, of the men (and sometimes the women) camped there with their rough bags of clothing, their plastic cups held out for whatever one may think to give them. Of Pioneer Square in Seattle, in a district once known as Skid Road, and which remains so for many; of a bench in the park there, beneath which I once saw a pool of blood. I think too of a woman with two small children whom I discovered one evening sheltered in a corner doorway in downtown Washington, and to whom I spoke and offered help. Because of my early experience, brief though it was, I have never been able to walk away from these people without giving them something, if no more than a dollar or two, a few coins. I understand, as the saying goes, that there, but for some saving grace, I might have been.

2002

Ginna

She was a slender, dark-haired girl who lived across the street from our house at Quarters N in the Washington Navy Yard at the end of the 1930s. Her name was Virginia, and she was the daughter and only child of Lieutenant Commander Adell, but we called her Ginna. The officers quarters in which she lived with her parents was the same house that the McHugh family lived in during an earlier period in the Yard. Sue McHigh and her older sister, Jeanne, had been close friends at the time, but no hint of romance ever intruded on our neighborly companionship. At the time of which I write, things were subtly different.

We were all Navy Yard kids, making the most of the confined space and facilities available to us. Except for an occasional family outing, a Sunday spent in the nearby Maryland or Virginia countryside, our lives were determined by the limitations imposed by the service life. Our city schoolmates inhabited another world, and except for an occasional school event to which we were all invited, our lives remained distant, remote from the normal city life. Every weekday morning we boarded a small bus parked and waiting at the fire station close to the main gate, and were driven uptown to our schools. The rest of the kids in the Yard went on to one of the district public schools; my younger brother, Bob, and I were enrolled at St. John's College, a Catholic school for boys with a certain amount of military training that was part of the school discipline. When the school day was over, our driver came to pick us up and return us to the Yard.

A major part of the Navy Yard was then known as the Naval Gun Factory, where much of our warships' armaments were manufactured. The old stone factory buildings were prominent in much of the Yard, and the workers came and went, morning and late afternoon, when the Yard whistle blew, walking the downhill street below our house. Precisely what my father's duties were at the time I can no longer be certain of. With the rank of commander and soon to be a captain, he disliked his periodic shore duty and much preferred to be at sea in one of his favorite submarines or another ship of the Pacific fleet. But our two-year stretch of Navy Yard life was a major respite from the continual shifting about, coast to coast, and we knew our mother looked forward to it.

Just when Ginna and I became something more than simply neighbors would be difficult to say now. There was, I think, from an early meeting something of a bonding between us that neither of us would have been able to articulate, and conventions of the time would likely have prevented any romance or intimacy between us. We all shared in certain events that were part of the Navy Yard social life: the occasional concerts, holiday parties, family gatherings, and the like.

I remember taking Ginna to a midwinter dance at a hotel in uptown Washington, an end-of-semester event sponsored by St. John's in the early years of World War II. At age sixteen, it may well have been a first date for me. I was shy, and romance was for me a fugitive thing of imagination, nourished by the books I had read and the Hollywood movies on view at the time. Nonetheless, and perhaps prompted by my parents, I approached Ginna and asked her for the date.

How well we danced that evening, I cannot recall. I can

still see the bright lights in the great ballroom of the hotel, and a few of my fellow students with their girlfriends, most of whom were no more sophisticated than I was in such circumstances. I remember my sense of confusion about what we were supposed to be doing out there on the dance floor, my arm around Ginna's waist, her head on my shoulder. Did we talk easily together? I can't say for certain, though I remember brief conversations with one or two of my classmates, and we may even have exchanged dance partners once or twice. It was, however, a major event in our lives at the time, and we were, if half secretly, excited about being there, taking part in the evening, listening to the music played by the orchestra hired for the occasion.

I had been given use of the family car for the evening, another first for both of us. After driving us back to the Yard late at night, I parked the car in front of Ginna's house where we exchanged a shy glance and a brief good-night kiss as we parted.

Thereafter the war increasingly intruded on public and private life. Our family left the Yard in early summer of 1941, bound west for Puget Sound, and Ginna as well as our other friends was left behind. Somehow she and I kept in sporadic touch over the next two or three years. In 1943 I was inducted into the Navy, leaving behind my senior year at Coronado High School. Following on early training in San Diego, I was shipped east to join a newly commissioned destroyer at the Boston Navy Yard. Ginna and her parents had by then moved to Boston, and while I was there she and I managed a brief meeting. Shortly before my ship was to leave for Panama and the Pacific, I called Ginna from a phone near the dock and she came to meet me there. What we had to say to each other I cannot be certain. I remember now something of a painful parting when I left her on the dock, boarded my ship, and watched her walk away.

During the wartime years that followed we exchanged

occasional letters, as she and her family moved from Boston to the West Coast, and then back to Washington. We were friends, and it was understood that we might meet again when the war was over and our families had settled. The letters we exchanged have not been saved, and I wonder now what I might have written to her from the Pacific War, and what she might have written to me. Though it was unspoken, there remained between us something more than a casual friendship.

With the war over, following on the surrender in Tokyo Bay and my release from Naval service some months later in San Diego, I returned to Washington to join my parents, then living at an address on Windom Place not far from the District line. My father had been assigned to shore duty at the Navy Department, and things were in a state of transition for all of us. Bob was still in the Navy, but would soon be discharged and return to California. After some hesitation, I had enrolled at what was then the National Art School, and began slowly to come to terms with my inclination to art, to painting and drawing, having realized that art, or something close to it, was to be a part of whatever new life I was entering.

It was not long after my return to Washington that Ginna and I began seriously to date again. I had by then bought a used car with my severance pay from the Navy, and I often drove out to Arlington in nearby Virginia, where Ginna was living with her parents. From time to time I took her out to a nightclub where we danced, this time with more confidence than we had on that one early occasion.

Among the certain memories of that time I recall one rather odd incident. Through the introduction of a friend, an ex-serviceman whom I met while traveling east, I discovered a weird old bar and café in an isolated area near the Potomac River known as Foggy Bottom, now occupied by the Pentagon. It was a smoky, rundown place at the end of a rough and muddy road, set off from the rest of the city by a soggy expanse of marshland,

and appeared to be something of a hangout for bohemians and others attracted to an unusual setting. The oddest feature of the place was a goat belonging to the owner of the bar. At any time of the evening it might be found wandering from table to table in search of a cigarette to chew, or standing up at the bar, looking for a glass of beer to drink. The animal was a part of the crowd, one of the family, a quiet and obedient creature in a scene like nothing else I ever found in Washington. I went there only occasionally, but it remained a special place, one reserved for an evening of drink and talk.

Meanwhile, my relationship with Ginna was growing more and more intense, though neither of us could say what it might lead to. Whether we talked at any length about my art studies I cannot say for certain, though we met from time to time at my school or at a nearby café for lunch or a cup of coffee. On weekends I drove out to Arlington to spend a few hours with her, and especially when for one reason or another her father was away. We sat downstairs until late in the evening, listening to music, caught up at times in a close embrace—"necking," as it was called—and becoming closer in our feeling for each other. One day that spring I took Ginna with me to the upper Potomac where I had been spending some of my weekend time fishing. Ginna seemed unsure of herself that day, wondering why it meant so much to me to be there. She watched me casting into the muddy current as she stood alone on the shoreline. And then it rained. We walked back to the car, wet and cold, Ginna complaining of the discomfort.

And one evening while we were together at her house, her mother, upstairs alone and apparently a little alarmed by our silence, called down to ask what we were doing, and to suggest that it was getting late and was time for me to leave. We had been lying together on the sofa, locked in each other's arms, Ginna astraddle my knee, and absorbed in long and passionate kissing. I think I may have attempted to undo her blouse, and

I can still remember her words to me, half whispered between our kisses: "Oh, Jack, Jack . . . . you make me so passionate!" I hardly knew what to do at the time; neither of us had yet allowed ourselves that final intimacy of sex, though we were getting close to it and sensed all too keenly the growing seriousness of our involvement and with no idea as to where it might take us.

Whether I discussed any of this with my parents, I cannot be certain. I think they understood that my relationship with Ginna was a serious matter, and they supported it as they always did anything I might do or hope to do.

As intense as things were between us at the time, our being together was still no more than intermittent, as school and other events claimed my time and energies as well as hers. Having spent our time together, I left her house late in the evening for the drive back to Windom Place. If we talked about our lives together, what we might do or make of our being together, I cannot now be certain. I had no realistic plans for our future, nor did she. Our being together was a kind of searching, underlain by something we felt to be serious, yet beyond definition. I was then twenty-two years old, still sorting out my school years and my wartime experience, serious about the art I was engaged in, yet unclear as to the direction my life might take. Ginna was perhaps a year or two younger. In her small, dark-haired frame and features I seemed to have found something I had dreamed of absently and could not have defined, yet there it was.

And then, suddenly, at the height of our involvement, came a phone call from Ginna one evening, telling me in a strained and tearful voice that she could not see me again. Her father had apparently become upset by our closeness, and the possible seriousness of it went counter to the plans he and her mother had for their daughter, which was, as I later learned, for her to marry into the Navy and continue the family tradition. I sensed in Ginna's voice, in what she had to tell me, that her father, now Captain

Adell, had punished her in some way, possibly with a beating, and had forced her to call me and give me the news. Listening to her, I did not know what to say or to do, but was more deeply stricken than I might have in any way been prepared for.

A short time later her parents called and arranged to have a meeting. By then my parents knew of the problem as I had been able to explain it to them, and they were both perplexed and angry. They had been aware of my affair with Ginna, had thought well of her, and were now concerned about me and the evident depression I had fallen into since getting her call.

Her mother and father arrived at our house on a Sunday afternoon in what appeared to be a rather forced friendly manner. We all sat in the living room with drinks, while Ginna's parents began their explanation of what had happened and why they had acted as they did. I listened, and quietly watched my parents becoming increasingly annoyed with the Adells as they explained that they felt that Ginna and I should not meet anymore, that our relationship, if continued, would not be good for either of us.

I can remember but one or two specific moments of that meeting. At one point Ginna's mother turned to my mother and asked her how she felt about it. And I heard my mother say to her, in an obviously angry tone of voice: "Well, I think they should be allowed to do what they want to do!" At that, Ginna's mother turned silent, while her father continued in his false and bantering tone. In a quieter moment, while they refreshed their drinks, he drew me aside and said in what he assumed was a confidential manner: "You know, you're going to be an artist, I understand, and you don't want a little person like Ginna cluttering up your life." And he said this with a sly smirk, as if, of course, I understood what he meant. I doubt that I said anything to him in reply; my silence throughout the meeting must have been obvious to everyone, as was the pain in my expression.

And then, with nothing more to say aside from a brief exchange of Navy gossip, the Adells got up to leave. The details of things thereafter are now mostly lost to me, but one moment following on that meeting remains clear. As we sat there in the room, the three of us in a depressed and angry mood, I heard my father say in an emphatic tone of voice: "Well, I hope I get him under my command someday—I'll make it hot for him!" That sensitivity, loyalty, and support on the part of both my father and mother is something I have never forgotten.

Some time after, I had a call from Ginna, asking to meet me at my school. The National Art School was then located on an upper floor of a large office building downtown. I met Ginna in the lobby of the building, where we stood for a few moments, finding it difficult to speak. I held her and we kissed, she in tears, telling me something of her father's treatment of her, and how bad she felt. She also told me that her mother had later confessed to her that, after their meeting with my family, she had felt that she and her husband may have been wrong in what they did, and that perhaps they should have left us alone. By then, however, it was too late, as we both realized. Our lives were already set in different directions, though I think neither of us could have defined any part of it. Ginna was now seeing a younger Navy man, or so I understood from that brief meeting.

I saw Ginna once more, on a Sunday afternoon at the Army-Navy Country Club in nearby Virginia. She was with a group of her friends and invited me to join them. But I had nothing to say to her, still sunk in a depressed, lovelorn mood. She was then more seriously involved with her Navy man, whom she probably married. I had no word of her afterward.

Later that summer I went with my mother to visit her sister, Aunt Kay, near Cleveland, Ohio. I had been asked to drive in the hope that the trip would take my mind off the affair with Ginna and relieve me of my all too obvious depression.

Few details of that long drive remain with me. We watched the Maryland, West Virginia, and Ohio countryside pass by, my mother and I engaged in intermittent conversation. Once we arrived at her sister's house in Lakewood, close to Lake Erie, my cousins and I were taken up in a family meeting, with talk and meals. Intent on a break from things, and possibly to help cheer me up, my uncle Joe and a friend of his invited me to accompany them on a short trip up Lake Erie into Canada. I did not know what lay in store for me, but soon found that we were on what turned out to be a five-day drunk.

Before heading north to Canada we stopped at a fairground outside the city, where the two older men for some reason insisted on having a try at a shooting gallery. The two of them had by then been drinking steadily, but I was still sober. When it came my turn, I stepped up to the counter, and with a .22 caliber rifle at my shoulder I proceeded to knock off every one of the ducks that were floating by at the far end of the gallery. My uncle, his friend, and the gallery owner stood by with their mouths open, astonished. I was myself surprised by my calm sense of purpose, but there was no doubt of my skill at shooting. After another round of drinks we left the fairground in a renewed good humor.

Moving north by ferry and highway into Canada, we stopped at a cheap and shabby motel near the lake. For the next three days the drinking continued, with jokes, pranks, and storytelling, and all to the obvious amusement of the motel owner. One moment of that time is still clear to me. There were no indoor toilets at the motel. One morning I went to the nearby outhouse to relieve myself. As I was sitting there I heard something crash with a loud noise against the outside wall of the privy. Alarmed, I jumped up from the seat and opened the door, to find my uncle standing not far away, laughing. He had thrown an empty bottle at the privy, just for the fun of it, knowing that I was inside. And that was the sort of bad-boy behavior I had to contend with during the brief holiday. I had realized that the whole adventure was one man's break from the home and office routine, apparently something the workhorse of the family needed from time to time.

And then, the fun time nearly over but while we were still fairly intoxicated, we boarded a ferry for the return to Cleveland. We arrived at my uncle's house in what I suspect was a rowdy and unshaven appearance, but in good humor, I still somewhat in shock at what I'd been involved in. My mother and I soon packed and left for the drive back to Washington. It had been a welcome visit, but the sadness was waiting for me when we returned to the house on Windom Place.

The remaining events of that summer are now mostly lost to me. I kept on with my art studies, with a break now and then for a trip to the Maryland or Virginia countryside, to fish or simply to be alone. The National Art School, meanwhile, had moved to a new location in a large redstone building not far from the Phillips Gallery in the Dupont area. The fall session was soon on its way, and I was once more absorbed in my artwork and all that it seemed to promise. I was still in recovery, but eventually became close friends with a young woman student, and little by little the pain left to me by Ginna and her parents faded into that tentative ground of a personal mythology.

Notes on the Contents

Original publication of the individual essays and reviews has been noted when possible.

The essay on Gilgamesh was delivered as a paper at an international literary conference in Atlanta, Georgia, 1999.

The paper on Jeffers was presented at a conference in Carmel, CA in 2000.

The review of *Postmodern Poetry* was written in 1994-95, and on request, date uncertain.

The review of *Rebel Angels* was published in *Sewanee Review*, in 1997.

"Some Thoughts on Poetry and the Call for Patriotism at this Time" was first published in the Jeffers *Tor House Newsletter*, Spring 2002.

"The Story of a Poem" was published in the *Hudson Review* in 1992, and written on request from the editor, Fred

Morgan, who had published the original poem in 1964, as noted.

"A Night on Cabin Creek" was written and revised in 2008.
Readings from *An Alaskan Journal* was first presented at Alaska Pacific University 1979.

John Haines contributed the foreword to Wayne Mergler's *The Last New Land: Stories of Alaska, Past and Present* (Anchorage: Alaska Northwest Books, 1996).

In *Book of the Tongass,* ANSCA stands for Alaska Native Claims Settlement Act.

The "Fate of a River" was published previously in *The Northern Line,* the newsletter of the Northern Alaska Environmental Center, Fairbanks, Alaska, April 1981.

"Forgotten Virtues" was originally published in a Sunday edition of the *Anchorage Daily News,* March 9, 2003.

"Fables and Distances: A Conversation with Alaska Writer John Haines" by John A. Murray was published in *Bloomsbury Review,* Denver, CO, date uncertain at this time.

John A. Murray, photographer and a contributing editor to the *Bloomsbury Review* has written or edited more than 40 books. He recently completed a new work of fiction, *One Hundred Stores,* and a collection of two dozen new essays, *Terra Nova.* He and John Haines have been friends since 1988.

The four "Poetry Chronicles" were published in the *Hudson Review,* on request by the editor. Chronicle I in Vol.

XLVIII, No. 4 (Winter 1996); Chronicle II in Vol. LIII, No. 4 (Winter 2001); Chronicle III in Vol. L, No. 2 (Summer 1997); Chronicle IV in Vol. LI, No. 3 (Autumn 1998).

Adam Kirsch's ("Poetry Chronicle IV") review of Adam Zagajewski's work appeared in *New Republis*, March 23, 1998.

"Wartime, a Late Memoir" was published in *Sewanee Review*, 2003.

"On the Street" was published in *Sewanee Review*, 2002.

"Ginna" was published in Sewanee Review, 2006.

OTHER BOOKS IN THE
NOTABLE VOICES SERIES

CAVANKERRY'S MISSION

Through publishing and programming, CavanKerry Press connects
communities of writers with communities of readers. We publish
poetry that reaches from the page to include the reader, by
the finest new and established contemporary writers. Our
programming brings our books and our poets to people
where they live, cultivating new audiences and
nourishing established ones.